A History of South Asia

ROBERT I. CRANE

513 AHA PAMPHLETS
AMERICAN HISTORICAL ASSOCIATION
400 A Street, SE, Washington, D.C. 20003

ROBERT I. CRANE is Ford-Maxwell Professor of South Asian History and director of the South Asia program at Syracuse University. His chief interests are modern South Asian history and nationalism, modernization, and social change in India. He received his B.A. from Duke University, his M.A. from American University, and his Ph.D. from Yale, and before coming to Syracuse in 1968 he taught at the University of Chicago, the University of Michigan, and Duke University. The author of numerous articles on the history of South Asia, he has also edited *Regions and Regionalism in South Asian Studies: An Exploratory Study* (Durham, 1967) and *Transition in South Asia: Problems of Modernization* (Durham, 1970). He has been editor of the *Journal of Asian Studies* and has been the recipient of numerous fellowships, including two from the American Council of Learned Societies. He was president of the Southeast Regional Conference on Asian Studies in 1970.

Earlier versions of this pamphlet, entitled The History of India: Its Study and Interpretation, *appeared in 1958 and 1965 in a series published by the Service Center for Teachers of History, affiliated with the American Historical Association. With the discontinuation of the Service Center, this series of AHA Pamphlets has been devised to replace the older series. The pamphlet as it is printed here has been entirely rewritten, and the bibliography has been brought up to date.*

© Copyright, THE AMERICAN HISTORICAL ASSOCIATION, 1958, 1965, 1973

All rights reserved. No part of this book may be reproduced in any form without permission in writing from the publisher, except by a reviewer who wishes to quote brief passages in connection with a review written for inclusion in a magazine or newspaper. The American Historical Association does not adopt official views on any field of history and does not necessarily agree or disagree with the views expressed in this book.

Standard Book Number: 0-87229-014-X
Library of Congress Catalog Card Number: 73-78930

Composed and printed at The William Byrd Press, Inc.
Richmond, Virginia 23228
Printed in the United States of America

A History of South Asia

ROBERT I. CRANE

Prologue

In 1958 it could be remarked that "a basic knowledge of the history of India is seldom available in the American college curriculum, while many of the significant publications in Indian history are hard to find in our libraries. Even more important is the fact that educated Americans tend to lack awareness of the framework of Indian history."[1] No one would pretend that substantial changes have been made in the past fifteen years in all aspects of the dismal picture then painted. Nonetheless, there have been changes, and those changes are relevant to the character of this essay.

To begin with, the development of serious South Asian studies, especially at the graduate level, has taken giant steps since 1958. Where in 1958 there were perhaps four centers for such studies, today there are at least twenty, and most of these are better

---

Space limitations do not permit a more exhaustive treatment of the topic than is sketched in these pages. No one would pretend that this brief essay could hope to do justice to so complex a subject as the study and interpretation of India's long history. It is hoped, however, that this introductory essay will point the way toward an appreciation of the framework for the serious study of India's past and of the conceptual problems involved. The titles suggested will help the reader to further informed inquiry and the creation of the basis for a sound comprehension of Indian society. In the last analysis it is not the wealth of information at hand that counts, but the use to which one puts the information. The term "India" has been used throughout the pamphlet to refer to the historical subcontinent, so-called prior to the Partition of 1947. "South Asia" refers to modern India, Pakistan, Ceylon, Nepal, and Bangladesh. I am deeply indebted to several Indian academic colleagues for insights upon which this essay rests.

[1] Robert I. Crane, *The History of India: Its Study and Interpretation*, Service Center for Teachers of History series, 17 (Washington, 1958; 2d ed., 1965), 1.

equipped and more sophisticated than were two of the four centers in 1958.

Moreover serious training in South Asian languages has gone forward substantially. In 1958, apart from courses in Sanskrit, there were no more than a handful of courses, with very small enrollments, in the languages of South Asia. Today South Asian languages are regularly taught on an intensive basis at a wide variety of colleges and universities in the United States. Enrollments have gone up by several hundred per cent during the past decade.

Change in the conditions of academic training has been accompanied by a very substantial development of South Asian library and research resources. In 1958 only the Library of Congress, the New York Public Library, and three or four university libraries were adequate for academic research on South Asia. Soon thereafter, as a result of the large-scale development of language- and area-studies programs and of the library program established by P.L. 480,[2] there was a major growth in scholarly library and research resources in a number of university libraries. In addition substantial microfilming projects have been undertaken in various archives, with the result that significant archival materials are now available. Through these measures the training of graduate students in South Asian studies and history has entered a new era.

All of these developments have been reflected in the quantity and quality of what has been published in the field of Indian history in this country during the past ten years. While a great deal remains to be done, the past decade has indeed been one of impressive progress and solid achievement, carrying with it considerable promise for the future. New questions have been posed, new issues probed, new dimensions explored, and new conceptual advances undertaken, all based on the slow but steady accumulation of empirical data upon which conceptualizations, hypotheses, and theory can be developed. The older, narrow reliance upon narrative, political history has been largely broken.

---

[2] For evaluative discussion of P.L. 480 collections on South Asia, see M. L. Patterson, "The South Asian P.L. 480 Library Program, 1962–1968," *Journal of Asian Studies*, 28 (1969): 143–54; and André Preibish, "Bibliographic Control of South Asian P.L. 480 Materials: An Automated Approach," *Journal of Asian Studies*, 31 (1972): 599–604.

Over one hundred years ago, in 1872, the publication of the first issue of *Indian Antiquary* signaled the beginning of what may be called professional historical studies of the subcontinent. The emphasis and focus were, however, on political and administrative history and the unraveling of dynastic records. That preoccupation has died slowly and only after exercising a disproportionate influence on our view of the history of the subcontinent. The past few years have witnessed new trends in historiography and the creation of a new framework for the viewing of Indian history. This essay seeks to reflect and advance that new viewpoint.

As this essay is designed to indicate, much hard and ingenious work remains, and a great deal of revision of what has been published in the past is needed, but there are few insurmountable problems, apart from the absence of reliable data, now facing the historian of South Asia. Two decades ago one could not have made that statement. At that time we were traveling over what was *terra incognita,* though far too many were blissfully ignorant of that fact. The result was the utterance of large generalizations and platitudes that acquired a spurious weight because they had been so often and so solemnly repeated. Most of them were, at best, half-truths often quite misleading and seldom of any heuristic value. During the past decade most of these hollow shibboleths have been seen for what they are—easy approximations to a truth that was largely hidden to those who had never known where or how to look.

Problems of Study and Interpretation

The study and writing of the history of India has been quite difficult for a variety of reasons, some of which are indigenous and some of which have been imported. One of the reasons has been the persistence, now beginning to give way, of basic gaps in our factual armory. One cannot write good history in the absence of an adequate base of factual knowledge. For certain periods, classes, or topics within the historical experience of the peoples of South Asia, we lack an acceptable factual base. For other periods, classes, or institutions we have data that are not agreed upon. Until our facts are in better order and important secular series have been assembled and verified, our ability to build middle-level theory and to test hypotheses will remain limited.

Quite apart from the problem of creating an adequate and relevant data base for the writing of Indian history are the problems of interpretation and conceptualization. Conceptualization sets the basis for and outlines the framework—conscious or subconscious—of reference that is essential in the effective writing of history. Europeans had a great deal to do with the creation and formulation of most of the traditions dominating Indian historiography until after the First World War. They tended to import, perhaps unintentionally, conceptualizations that had been developed in the writing of the history of Europe. These conceptualizations could, of course, lead to bias and distortion in the selection of factual information as well as in the interpretation of India's past. The most recent decade has been important in Indian historiography because historians are facing up to these issues on a professional basis at last. The result has been a major effort at reinterpretation, accompanied by the flux that is part of a long overdue effort of this sort.

Major sources of misinterpretation, or of bias in interpretation, marked a great deal of the history of the subcontinent published before World War II. These need to be suggested before turning to elements of a new schema and a fresh overview. The first significant source of interpretive bias from which the writing of Indian history in the past has suffered—and which has affected interpretation in several potentially adverse ways—has been the Eurocentric models that have been taken for granted by so many of those who have written Indian history. The British occupation of India carried with it the assumption, by most Europeans and not a few Indians and Americans, that European conventions, European ways of viewing the past, European values, and European concepts of linear or evolutionary development were the norm and that all other societies must, consciously or unconsciously, be fitted to such Eurocentric norms. In its most complete forms, this was cultural imperialism in extravagant lineaments. At the more naive level, this meant that if there had been a medieval period or a dark age in Europe, then of course India, too, must have passed through its own dark age or its own medieval period. If Europe had experienced feudalism, India too must have undergone a "feudal" age, and so on.³ If England were deemed great because it was proclaimed the "Mother of Parliaments," then many a patriotic scholar in India, who desired to find that his own society had also been great, was obliged to discover that archaic India had been the scene of countless village republics—while European writers pegged India several levels down the Social Darwinist evolutionary scale because they could find no parliaments in India's past.

Englishmen of different schools of thought did, of course, see India's past in a variety of ways. As so often happens in the writing of history, the history of South Asia was to be found in the eye of the beholder.⁴ The same set of facts was interpreted differently, depending upon the intellectual, religious, economic, political, or other preferences of the individual who happened to be writing. More important, the needs of different periods affected the way in which the British viewed their greatest imperial dependency and hence the ways in which British authors tended to interpret Indian society and Indian history. Thus David Kopf has argued persuasively that as long as Englishmen with predominantly cosmopolitan outlooks and sympathetic viewpoints were in the ascendancy in official circles in nineteenth-century Calcutta, cultural and intellectual collaboration was maximized and India's past was optimistically viewed as worthy of study. As soon as an invidious policy of Westernization replaced the cosmopolitan Hinduphilia of the earlier group, in the years 1828–35, collaboration declined and "cultural barricades of nationalism were hastily erected."⁵ The immediate result was the rise of traditionalism among Bengali intellectuals and the growth of anti-Hindu sentiment among the European ruling class in India. This in turn led to a new interpretation, at least for the time being, of India's past, an interpretation that rested upon the authority of James Mill's *History of British India,* first published in London in 1817, a later edition

---

³ For a thoughtful discussion, see Daniel Thorner, "Feudalism in India," in Rushton Coulborn, ed., *Feudalism in History* (Princeton, 1956), 133–50.

⁴ See, for example, George Bearce, *British Attitudes towards India, 1784–1858* (London, 1961), for major trends in British opinion. See also A. J. Greenberger, *The British Image of India* (London, 1969), which focuses upon changes in British ideas about India in three successive eras of the imperial connection.

⁵ David Kopf, "The Brahmo Samaj Intelligentsia and the Bengal Renaissance," in Robert I. Crane, ed., *Transition in South Asia: Problems of Modernization* (Durham, 1970), 7–48.

appearing in 1834. This was one of the most influential histories written before World War I. Its interpretation, based upon Utilitarian ideas, was by no means sympathetic to Indian culture or society. For several decades after 1835 the Utilitarians played a prominent role in the civil administration of British India and did what they could to transform and reform Indian society and institutions along lines approved by Utilitarian thought.[6] Utilitarians were scarcely inclined to credit India's past and traditions—or any traditions—with much, if any, virtue. Most of them sought to import rapid progress by changing the habits and motivations of a people whose way of life they frowned upon. This viewpoint, buttressed by Mill's highly respected history, led to a new phase in the European view of India's past. T. B. Macaulay epitomized that view when he publicly scoffed at Oriental texts that would "provoke mirth" in an English boarding school for young girls.

This harsh view, by the way, easily became the intellectual handmaid of imperialists and missionaries alike. If the people of India were sunk in ignorance, superstition, and sloth, the imperial administrator could the more easily take pride in having "rescued" his subjects from so degraded a condition, while the missionary could thank Divine Providence for the opportunity to lift the heathen from so cursed a plight. Now that schools were being opened for the "improvement" of the "natives," self-interest suggested that Her Majesty's subjects be reminded of the pathetic conditions in which their British masters had found them so that they would not fail to appreciate how much their "guardians" were doing for them. If by chance this "improvement" were to conduce to the "natives'" conversion to Christianity, so much the better.[7] At the same time the new rulers could, directly or indirectly, point out how superior British rule was to the benighted and oppressive rule of the Oriental "despots" whom they had replaced. This theme, which came to be quite prominent in the

[6] Eric Stokes, *The English Utilitarians and India* (Oxford, 1959), traces the Utilitarian influences on policy in India. For a searching inquiry into the effects of Utilitarian doctrines on the Indian rural order, see Ravinder Kumar, *Western India in the Nineteenth Century* (London, 1968).

[7] It should be kept in mind that the administrators, by and large, had no special interest in the propagation of Christianity, though many were committed to the improvement of the condition and customs of their native subjects. Our concern is with the implications of such views for the writing of India's history.

historiography of India after the Mutiny of 1857, not only served to justify British rule as immeasurably better than native rule but also—perhaps as an unintentional by-product—intimated that the Muslim rulers of India, from whom Britain had wrested the scepter, had been a particularly rapacious lot, ever ready to mulct or mistreat their Hindu subjects. This lesson in Indian history, the goal of which was to make British rule appear in a more favorable light, exacerbated animosities between the Hindu and Muslim communities.[8]

A second prolific source of bias and misinterpretation in the writing of South Asian history has been its polemic character. Because India was a British possession for one hundred and fifty years, it was long an object of controversy. In the early period the East India Company had to fight to protect its monopoly against a variety of interlopers and contenders. The growth of political economy in Western Europe was in no small measure enriched by the controversies that raged over the status of the East India Company's monopoly in the trade and political dominance of India or over the propriety of Britain's special position in the subcontinent.[9]

Later, during the rise of active Evangelical efforts, contending schools of thought published a hearty polemical and pamphlet literature discussing how missionary endeavor should proceed or the merits of efforts to Christianize the heathen. This literature involved several versions of Indian society and various opinions of India's past. By this time a controversy had already emerged between the Hinduphiles and the Hinduphobes, as Kopf has dubbed them, or the Orientalists and the Anglicists, who took opposing positions with regard to the evaluation of India's cultural contributions and India's traditions.[10] The Orientalists, generally speaking, saw India's past as having involved a Golden Age, followed to be sure by a Dark Age in which pristine Aryan institu-

---

[8] The vernacular press of the period from 1875 to 1900 contains repeated references to English textbooks in the Indian syllabus that taught this version of Muslim rule and commented upon its adverse consequences.

[9] See, for example, the fine article by Joseph Spengler, "India's Prospects according to Jean-Baptiste Say," *Journal of Asian Studies*, 28 (1969): 595–600.

[10] David Kopf, *British Orientalism and the Bengal Renaissance* (Berkeley, 1969). See also the view of the Muslim in Percival Spear, *India, A Modern History* (Ann Arbor, 1961). The Orientalist view receives its most scholarly presentation in A. L. Basham, *The Wonder That Was India* (New York, 1954).

tions had ossified and become overlaid with superstitions and degrading practices. These episodes, it was held, had so reduced Hindu society from its former exalted condition as to permit outside barbarians, of whom the Muslims were but the final examples, to invade and humiliate. From this blight Britain had rescued the poor Hindu, and *Pax Britannica* had allowed him to be resuscitated. A renaissance could now take place, and Hindu society, under benign British tutelage, could once again be restored to an approximation of its former glories.

When the Mutiny of 1857 erupted, a fresh and virulent polemical battle took place among several groups of Britains, each of whom blamed the other for the debacle, somewhat like the futile struggle in the United States over what was called the "loss of China" in the 1950s. Each group in Britain hoped, if it could successfully lay the blame at the door of another group, to gain differential benefits during the post-Mutiny settlement. Retrospectively, after the Mutiny had been suppressed, new lines of policy for the administration of the Indian Empire had to be drawn up, and the policy-makers had to take decisions about the causes of the Mutiny so as to arrange the affairs of the subcontinent in such a manner as to avert or minimize the possibility of another outbreak. The reading of India's past came to be important to administrators in deciding how to manage its future with maximum security for British rule.[11] As two later historians of British India have remarked, with regard to the historiography of the Mutiny and its aftermath:

Many important official documents and some recent histories were written, consciously or unconsciously, with an eye to certain criticisms

[11] Continuing controversy exists over the causes of the Mutiny, its nature, its scope, and how its recurrence was best to be averted. The Mutiny remained a preoccupation with the British in India for a full half century after it had been suppressed and influenced the policy of the government for at least that span of time. Voluminous publications, from 1857 down to the present day, attest to the significance with which it was viewed, the controversy it attracted, and the diverse conclusions produced by those who have written about it. It was the subject of parliamentary debate and inquiry as well as polemic broadsides. Indian nationalists have often viewed it as the "first war of Indian independence," while many British authors argue it was a military outbreak only. See S. N. Sen, *Eighteen Fifty-Seven* (Delhi, 1957); W. H. Russell, *My Indian Mutiny Diary* (republished; London, 1957); S. B. Chaudhuri, *Civil Rebellion in the Indian Mutiny* (Calcutta, 1957); and Ainslie Embree, *1857 in India* (Boston, 1963), which presents extracts from contrasting interpretations.

which have been made in India or abroad. The growth of Indian nationalism has accentuated a bias which is often unfavorable to Indians. . . .

The mischievous tendency to make historical truth subservient to administrative expediency has been increased by changes in legal practice and procedure, which operate as an effective censorship. . . . The freedom with which the Mutiny was discussed during the subsequent two decades would have led, under present conditions, to innumerable *causes célèbres*. . . . Official secretiveness, of which there was little before the Mutiny, combined with this informal censorship, makes it almost impossible to supply the "penetration, accuracy, and coloring" which Dr. Johnson demanded of the historian.[12]

A major consequence of the Mutiny was the overt search for allies upon whose support the security of British rule could be based. This led to differences of opinion and divergent policy prescriptions among imperial civil servants and senior administrators, the one consistent theme being the effort to locate allies whose support would ensure the stability and enhance the longevity of Crown rule in India. To some policy-makers this meant reliance upon the Muslim minority, who could be cultivated to keep the Hindu majority off balance, while other officials decried a policy of favoritism or argued that the Muslims were unreliable. Some administrators viewed the aristocrats and "princes" as the natural allies of the British raj, or rule, while others held out for policies that would favor the peasant, especially the yeoman farmer.[13] The post-Mutiny era (1858–1907) was one in which the British interpretation of India's past underwent revision under the impact of the Mutiny and its policy implications. Post-Mutiny authors tended to view the Muslims in a generally more favorable light, the aristocrats as Britain's friends, and the yeoman class as

---

[12] Edward Thompson and G. T. Garratt, *Rise and Fulfillment of British Rule in India* (Allahabad, 1958), vii–viii.

[13] The paradoxes of the period of Crown rule, especially the half century after the Mutiny, have been increasingly explored in the past few years. What is still lacking is effective evaluation of Indian responses and indigenous movements, which the British but dimly comprehended. For the formation of the British view and policies, see H. L. Singh, *Problems and Policies of the British in India, 1885–1898* (London, 1963); T. R. Metcalf, *The Aftermath of Revolt: India, 1857–1870* (Princeton, 1964); Sarvepalli Gopal, *British Policy in India, 1858–1905* (Cambridge, 1965); N. G. Barrier, *The Punjab Alienation of Land Bill of 1900* (Durham, 1966); and C. H. Philips, ed., *The Evolution of India and Pakistan, 1858 to 1947: Select Documents* (London, 1962).

the backbone of India's society. In this period emerged the myth of the Indian Civil Service as a *corps d'élite* of "guardians"[14] whose task it was to govern India on the principle of *noblesse oblige*, without favoritism or involvement in the crass and petty concerns of the countinghouse or "politics." The civil servants were to be above partisanship and were to vouchsafe to the masses those things that were best for them, whether the masses were capable of appreciating it or not. Answerable only to the governor-general and to the secretary of state for India in Westminster, the "Heaven-born," as they were often called, were to provide good government instead of anything like self-government. In this they expressed the colonialist mentality in its most highly developed and elitist form, though they reflected a set of attitudes evident among many who were charged with the governing of England itself.

Partisan strife led almost imperceptibly into the conflict that grew between the nascent Indian nationalists and their British rulers, as the latter sought to exculpate and justify while the former sought to indict and convict. Rarely have two parties been in more basic disagreement over the interpretation of what was, in effect, the same historical record, for each camp selected certain sets of facts from the total repertoire and drew its own interpretation from the facts it had selected. Each decade the debate grew more acrid and the positions of the antagonists more irreconcilable.

Concomitantly, the variant readings of history diverged ever more widely. In the 1880s the early constitutional nationalists, seeking little more than a share of the power the British had for so long monopolized, enunciated the blessings of British rule and averred their desire to fulfill their role as loyal British subjects. But by 1920 Gandhi could speak of "satanic" British rule. Just a few years before that the cult of the bomb had spread in a vain terrorist attempt to drive the hated British raj from India. Meanwhile both sides rewrote Indian history to suit their purposes, with more heat than light, producing a profound and noxious effect on most aspects of the writing of Indian history. The inter-

---

[14] This is what Philip Woodruff entitled the second volume of his history of the Indian Civil Service, written at the suggestion of retired members of the service. *The Men Who Ruled India* (New York, 1954).

pretation of the place and role of Islam in India was also distorted, because of the importance of communal relations to the development of nationalism, to British colonial policy, and to the political evolution of the subcontinent.

The British did not create communalism in the subcontinent: its virus was there before the British spread their dominion. But it cannot be overlooked that colonial policy intensified communal tensions and helped to create new arenas in which communalism could flourish. Moreover, elements of the British interpretation of India's history lent themselves to communalism, as, for example, criticism in British textbooks of the alleged tyrannies of Muslim rulers encouraged Hindu resentment of Muslims. The growth of the communal spirit and communal politics after 1857 facilitated the development of communalist interpretations of India's history. Communal groups and communal political parties—Hindu, Muslim, and Sikh—sought justification for their points of view and their policies in communalist versions of their own past or of the past of the rival communities. Some of the most strident of the polemical literature published in India after 1880—often inciting to riot—was communal history or communal politics, and the line between the two was frequently difficult to draw.[15]

A third and more subtle form of bias in the interpretation of South Asian history has been the subconscious emphasis upon the

[15] There is a spate of communal literature, much of it fugitive in character, but all too little scholarly analysis. For good recent studies of the communal element in historical writings, see Romilla Thapar, Harbans Mukhia, and Bipan Chandra, *Communalism and the Writing of Indian History* (Delhi, 1969); N. G. Barrier, "The Arya Samaj and Congress Politics in the Punjab, 1894–1908," *Journal of Asian Studies*, 26 (1967): 363–79; N. G. Barrier, "The Punjab Government and Communal Politics, 1870–1908," *Journal of Asian Studies*, 27 (1968): 523–39; and K. W. Jones, "Communalism in the Punjab," *Journal of Asian Studies*, 28 (1968): 39–54. See also, for an incisive analysis of the role of the government in exacerbating communalism, J. H. Broomfield, *Elite Conflict in a Plural Society: Twentieth Century Bengal* (Berkeley, 1968). For a related aspect, by an author whose aim was not the propagation of communalism but whose writings had that effect, see the article by T. W. Clark, "The Role of Bankimcandra in the Development of Nationalism," in C. H. Philips, ed., *Historians of India, Pakistan and Ceylon* (London, 1961), 429–45; and, in the same volume, the essay by R. C. Majumdar, "Nationalist Historians," pp. 416–28. For an Indian view, which holds the "divide-and-rule" tactics of the British largely responsible for the growth of communalism, see M. N. Das, *India under Morley and Minto* (London, 1964), and the excellent analyses in Gopal Krishna, "Religion in Politics," *Indian Economic and Social History Review*, 8 (1971): 362–94.

history of the British in India rather than upon the indigenous peoples of the subcontinent. In addition, until the past few years the tendency has been to write about those topics and issues interesting to the governing bureaucracy and the commercial or missionary expatriates. This tendency was, of course, facilitated by the fact that the bureaucracy, which administered India, kept the records and compiled the archives. Research was therefore easier on those topics the officials deemed important. But this was a relatively narrow range of topics, and, even worse, it was viewed from the official and the European vantage point and in terms of official preoccupations and official sources. All too often the officials—or for that matter the commercial agents and missionaries—had no more than a faint inkling of what the indigenous viewpoint or structure of social action might be. All too frequently in the contact between European and Indian the two parties were talking past each other because the meanings behind the words were basically different.[16] This led, of course, to unexpected and unforeseen misunderstandings, but more important it caused different versions of "reality" to appear to the parties who seemed to be engaged in a dialogue. At the same time the tendency to concentrate upon the topics that formed the preoccupations of the officials gave to the published histories the aura of official presentations even when they were not apologia, as they often were.

Insofar as Indian authors, particularly nationalist writers, increased the stridency of their criticisms of British rule—as was largely true after World War I—British authors tended, by a natural defensive measure, to close ranks in self-protection, thus increasing the disposition to see things "through British eyes" and to interpret the historical record in a light at times unconsciously

---

[16] Frantz Fanon, *The Wretched of the Earth* (New York, 1963), has provided a stimulating and most persuasive analysis of the inability of the colonists to comprehend the milieu and the value system of the colonized. But see also the excellent article by Walter C. Neale, in which it is shown that the British administrators meant very different things by land ownership than did their Indian predecessors. "Land Is To Rule," in R. E. Frykenberg, ed., *Land Control and Social Structure in Indian History* (Madison, 1969), 3–16. Ainslie Embree makes the same point even more specifically in another paper in the same volume, "Landholding in India and British Institutions," pp. 33–52.

favorable to British rule.[17] This bias has had its counterpart, among Indians, in a bias in favor of a range of topics of interest to the literate elite and the affluent class. This class was during British rule the one and one-half per cent of the population that sought to share power with the colonial rulers and blossomed as literati, professional men, subordinate government servants, journalists, and bourgeois trade-union leaders. Unable to secure more than a meager handful of crumbs from the British table, the new Indian middle class became increasingly militant and insistent upon self-rule. The gap between them and the illiterate and poor masses in the rural countryside, however, was about as great as was the gap between the officials of the raj and the peasants. The coming of independence changed the government and the rhetoric, but the range of interests exhibited by historical writing is not much broader or deeper today than it was twenty-five years ago, and any expansion of range that has taken place is due at least partly to the development of disciplines such as anthropology, sociology, and social psychology, which have caused professional academics to look in new places for data and to utilize new conceptual schemes in ordering the data uncovered.

The pronounced Eurocentric bias has affected the problem of periodization, which would in any event have been difficult. For a long time schemes of periodization drawn from European history were simply lifted baldly and applied, on the basis of apparent analogy, to India's past. Unworkable even in the best of circumstances, this sort of conceptual transplant breaks down quickly over the fact that what might work for Bengal or the Punjab will not work for Maharashtra or the Karnatak. The cycle of historical time and institutional development in the Chola area was quite different from the cycle of historical time in the kingdoms of the Ganges Delta. India's past has involved several different regional identities, and each regional tradition has had its own past, its own periodization (of course influenced by its neighbors),

---

[17] E. M. Forster's fine novel, *A Passage to India* (1924), deals in good part with the British ruling group in India and the ways in which their preconceptions prevented most of them from seeing reality in the same way as it was experienced by their Indian subjects. His volume becomes, as it were, a commentary on the Whorfian hypothesis.

its own major language and literature, its own dynasties, and its own customs and institutions. The past few years have witnessed serious efforts at systematic study of more than one of these regional identities as well as of the underlying phenomena involved in regionalism.[18] The subcontinent is, in a sense, not unlike Europe west of Russia, and the writing of its history presents problems of organization that are in certain respects not dissimilar to those faced in organizing a history of Western Europe. India has fourteen major indigenous languages, each of which has at least ten million native speakers, a situation comparable to that we find in Europe.

In addition, the topography, climate, and geomorphology of India are highly diversified. Physical extremes of terrain and climate are nowhere more prominent than here. Deserts, swampy deltas, high mountains, alluvial plains, glaciers, arid wastes, and upland meadows are all part of the Indian physical heritage. Such great variety in the physical environment has had its impact upon the peoples and the varieties of their cultural and historical experiences. The viewpoints brought in from European history, however, failed adequately to prepare the student of the Indian setting for the complexity of South Asian geography.

During historic times it appears that the patterns of climate, rainfall, and meterology we know today were much the same, though subject to local variation. Since 300 B.C. we know of no substantial changes in climate, flora, or fauna, except for the Thar Desert in northwest India, which has been spreading eastward at a slow pace. With the clearing of the forest by human effort, there has also been a steady decline of wildlife, and certain species are now almost extinct.

It should be noted that the Deccan Plateau in the south is largely cut off from the great alluvial Ganges Plain in the north by the spiny Vindhya Mountains, which limited the movement of peoples between the peninsula and North India. One obvious

---

[18] Robert I. Crane, ed., *Regions and Regionalism in South Asian Studies: An Exploratory Study* (Durham, 1967); S. P. Sen, ed., *Studies in Modern Indian History: A Regional Survey* (Calcutta, 1969). A substantial amount of material scattered in scholarly journals is now concerned with manifestations of regional tradition or regional identity. See also studies of institutions in their regional settings, such as William E. Reinhardt, *The Legislative Council of the Punjab, 1897-1912* (Durham, 1972).

consequence of this is that the Indo-Aryan, or Sanskritic, languages lie predominantly to the north, while the so-called Dravidian languages are found in peninsular and South India.

Moreover, the subcontinent is cut off in the northeast and north by very forbidding mountain ranges, the Himalayan and Hindu Kush. Passes penetrate these ranges, and peoples have infiltrated through them, but they are not easy means of access. Most important, the ranges have sheltered the subcontinent from the climate of Siberia and Tibet and played a role in the circulation of the Indian monsoon winds and moisture within the ecosystem of the subcontinent.

One way of viewing the significant features of the geography of South Asia, apart from those broad features just mentioned, has been offered by the geographer W. M. Day, who distinguishes three types of regions, each of which is said to have had a distinctive influence.[19] Day uses the term "nuclear" for the major river basins and their important adjacent agricultural areas. These rich and stable zones of production have maintained their cultural continuity and identity over long centuries. Such stable areas fill virtually all the prerequisites for large-scale state formation and the support of a leisure class that can propagate a high intellectual tradition as well as support trade and commerce. The second type is defined as the shatter zone, or route area, through which peoples passed in migratory movements or invasions on repeated occasions. These zones connected the great nuclear areas and contained no permanent political or cultural traditions but reflected a cultural mosaic. A subtype of the shatter zone is the marcher, or border, area, a relatively unstable transition zone between the hills and the plains. The third major type of region is called the cul-de-sac, or region of relative isolation. Here, due to eco-traits that minimize access, pockets of people have tended to be bypassed. These zones would include areas in the uplands of Central India or the Himalayan tribal areas described by G. D. Berreman in his *Hindus of the Himalayas*.[20]

---

[19] W. M. Day, "Relative Permanence of Former Boundaries in India," *Scottish Geographical Magazine*, 65 (1949): 113–22. See also Crane, *Regions and Regionalism in South Asian Studies*, and Norton Ginsberg, ed., *The Pattern of Asia* (Englewood Cliffs, 1968).

[20] G. D. Berreman, *Hindus of the Himalayas* (Berkeley, 1963), 430.

Much of the literature on the cultural geography and regional variations of South Asia suggests an intimate but by no means rigid relationship between cultural patterns and geographical-ecological features. This kind of relationship is apparent if one considers the incidence of the annual monsoon. When more than eighty-five per cent of the rain falls within two and one-half summer months, there are bound to be considerable effects upon patterns of habitation, agricultural practices, systems of water conservancy, the role of administration, land-man ratios, and so forth. In an early and technologically unsophisticated age, problems of water management dominated many aspects of rural life (they are still of great importance today) and preoccupied the people and their rulers. In the absence of any mechanical system for moving water and with a dearth of nonhuman motive power, a significant share of the rural population had to be involved during the growing season in the daily task of moving water from storage areas out to the fields or in the repair of water channels. In recent years advanced technology has changed this situation, sharply reducing the amount of human labor power required, vastly improving water conservancy measures, and expediting the flow of water to the fields. The terms under which man interacts with nature have changed, and this has had observable effects on patterns of living and work. Similar changes in man's interaction with environment may well have been significant in the development of Hindu society throughout its long and checkered history.

The existence of major historical regions, languages, and cultures—and the existence of topographical diversity—in South Asia posed very real difficulties for those who attempted to write Indian history. Authors have frequently made reference to "unity in diversity," but the phrase, which exemplified one way of viewing India's past, tends to beg the question. As posed, it does not aid the student in uncovering the regularities that may be there or the processes at work that help to govern the interaction between the unity posed and the diversity recognized. Nor does the phrase suggest at which levels we may expect to find the unity and at which the diversity. The phrase "unity in diversity" refers not only as convenient shorthand to the regional, cultural, and linguistic traditions that have coexisted in India for more than a thousand years, but also to the diversity of ethnic types that have invaded India from the north and northwest during the past two thousand years. Each such ethnic group brought into the subcontinent its own distinctive cultural contribution, life-style, folkways, and dialect or language. India's past has not been characterized by what we know as the "melting-pot" philosophy, and as a result each separate way of life or pattern of behavior has tended to persist with only modest modifications.

Though it has been argued that the lower social groups may have sought to improve their status by emulating portions of the life-style of superior social classes, this does not constitute convincing evidence that anything like wholesale acculturation has taken place between such classes prior to the present century. Parochialism, moreover, has long tended to keep customs and patterns of behavior that were the norm in one region or social class from spreading much beyond traditional cultural, social, linguistic, or other boundaries. Such facts call into question some of the implications of the theme of "unity in diversity," so widely mentioned in the published histories.

The stratification and parochialism inherent in a society organized around the hierarchical caste system materially reinforced the tendency of traditional Indian society to minimize acculturation between the various regions and ethnic groups. For long centuries each endogamous caste, governed in its patterns of behavior by its caste oligarchy, lived under the customary rules handed down from the past. Change and acculturation could not be prevented (and in the past hundred years such change has been at an accelerating pace), but over many decades change was minimized, and thus the unique features of many dozens of parochial "little traditions" were preserved.

For centuries, as Burton Stein has pointed out, the basic form of organization in the sociopolitical life of the subcontinent was what has been termed a territorially segmented unit, based upon the overlapping existence of fundamental social organizational forms and loyalties, marriage networks, kinship ties, caste affiliations, associated economic arrangements, and "political" or territorial boundaries. In such forms of organization, based upon the coexistence of what Clifford Geertz once called "primordial loyalties," social, structural, jural, associational, and normative traditions—all parochial in nature—marched together to maintain the cohesion and the tradition of the group and to minimize the influx of alien ways of doing things.[21] Within each such territorially segmented unit there are, of course, hierarchy, the caste system, class relationships, and so forth. One of these units may appear on the surface to be very much like a unit nearby, but in fact the structure, myths, rules of intragroup interactions, jural relations, system of taboos, and rules governing marriage and descent may be quite different from one unit to the next. The principalities and jurisdictions of the magnates, as well as the kingdoms erected upon the shoulders of these lesser chieftains, have throughout India's long history proliferated, waxed and waned in number, and separated the subcontinent into a bewildering variety of levels of political jurisdictions in which, by a peculiarly Indian trait, caste has normally not extended its endogamous boundaries beyond the borders of the state or principality in which its natal homestead was to be found.

Each region has had its own parochial market and artisan castes, exchange arrangements, and power brokers. According to orthodox Hindu belief the chieftain or king was responsible for maintaining orthodoxy and, especially, for settling and maintaining the purity and stability of the castes in his jurisdiction. In practice this seems to have meant not infrequently that the local ruler more or less decided upon the caste hierarchy in his domain, normally with the advice of his Brahman coadjutor, and settled most intercaste disputes.[22]

Religion is another source of diversity, though in at least one of its dimensions, of unity as well. But a sound understanding of its role in promoting unity is still not possible, for it is not clear how far high Brahmanical Hinduism, or let us say, Neo-Vedanta Hinduism, actually goes in providing a unifying ideational, cultural, and ethical system for the 450 million Hindus.

[21] Burton Stein, "Brahman and Peasant in Early South Indian History," *Adyar Library Bulletin*, 31–32 (1967–68): 229–69; Clifford Geertz, "The Integrative Revolution: Primordial Sentiments and Civil Politics in the New States," in Chicago Committee for the Comparative Study of New Nations, *Old Societies and New States*, ed. Clifford Geertz (New York, 1963), 105–57.

[22] There are extant late-nineteenth-century records of Indian rulers determining the caste hierarchy and precedence within their small states.

This is true for several reasons. To begin with, Hinduism is not and never has been an organized credal faith with anything like a central source of doctrinal authority or orthodoxy. Nor does it have a single sacred book like the Koran or the Bible. On the contrary there is a far-flung and diffuse sacerdotal class, the Brahman priesthood, loosely organized around a network of "schools" and virtually autonomous and self-regulating temples. Moreover there are several major and additional minor orders of sannyasis, or holy men, each of which has its own independent existence. Some of these priests and sannyasis are attached by prebendal grants to one or another of the innumerable temples and temple schools, or maths, which dot the land, but many Brahmans hold a hereditary living, which they may or may not choose to occupy, as the priest of a certain village. It is not at all easy to know what portion of the vast body of Sanskritic, hieratic lore the thousands of priests, astrologers, and wandering ascetics, or other varieties of Brahman religious specialists and technicians—individually and collectively—share or would agree upon. There is probably no more loosely organized priestly body of knowledge extant anywhere in the world. In addition there have been a wide variety of sects, each with its own founder and its own doctrines.

Each caste of Brahmans, each region, and each principality had its own version or recension of Brahmanical texts that were, to a greater or lesser extent, diffused among ritually clean, respectable non-Brahman clients. But we know far too little about the extent to which and the effectiveness with which the high Brahmanical traditions were diffused among non-Brahmans to modify the little folk and parochial traditions. M. N. Srinivas has proposed that this diffusion, which he calls Sanskritization, was continuous, far-reaching, and effective. But his view has been challenged, and anthropologists and cultural historians have reported village folk with vigorous local and particularist traditions little influenced by the classical, Brahmanical system.[23] At best the situation in India's 550,000 villages remains unclear.

In addition there are Islam, Sikhism, Jainism, Neo-Buddhism,

---

[23] M. N. Srinivas, "A Note on Sanskritization and Westernization," *Far Eastern Quarterly*, 15 (1956): 481–96. Those who have challenged the view held by Srinivas include J. F. Staal, "Sanskrit and Sanskritization," *Journal of Asian Studies*, 22 (1963): 261–76; and R. J. Miller, "Button, Button . . . Great Tradition, Little Tradition, Whose Tradition?" *Anthropological Quarterly*, 39 (1966): 26–41.

tribal animist religions, and Christianity. Each of these religions can claim at least two million believers in the Republic of India, and all of them add to intellectual and cultural diversity. Each religious group tends to promote its own version of India's past.

In the midst of all of this, the re-creation of South Asian history has been concerned with issues, problems, categories, and topics handed down from the past or imported into the understanding of India by Orientalists, Sanskritists, or by Utilitarians, Hinduphobes, or Anglicists. Much of what the nineteenth-century authors taught us, for reasons touched upon, has now to be abandoned, revised, or brought into serious question. At the very least, South Asian history must be conceptualized and written from an indigenous point of view, as the history of India or of Pakistan and not as the history of the European in India.

Other biases in the published literature include the persistent emphasis in favor of North India, or Hindustan, as contrasted with South India. This emphasis has accompanied the bias, already mentioned, in favor of narrative political history at the expense of other kinds of history and an undue reliance upon the "greatman" approach to the writing of history, with its many volumes on various emperors, kings, viceroys, adventurers, generals, political leaders, and the occasional eccentric, or holy man.[24]

There is yet another topic that has not been dealt with adequately. During the most recent decades India has experienced a considerable degree of modernization, at an accelerating pace,

[24] This stress upon the lives of "great men" is in part a reflection of the lack of understanding or comprehension of social process and events among the great mass of the people. Eurocentric preoccupations and the failure to understand the concerns of the mass of the people led inevitably to an undue emphasis upon biographies of kings and viceroys, about whom data would be easier to grasp and manipulate. Now that social sciences have begun to interact with the new history, we can see a change away from this preoccupation with "great men." New kinds of inquiry lead to new sources, which enable historians to turn to different topics and to concern themselves with process and social change. See, for example, Bernard Cohn, *India: The Social Anthropology of a Civilization* (Englewood Cliffs, 1971); Thomas Kessinger, "Historical Materials on Rural India," *Indian Economic and Social History Review*, 7 (1970): 489–510; Burton Stein, "Coromandel Trade in Medieval India," in John Parker, ed., *Merchants and Scholars: Essays in the History of Exploration and Trade* (Minneapolis, 1965), 49–60; Burton Stein, "Integration of the Agrarian System of South India," in Frykenberg, *Land Control and Social Structure in Indian History*, 175–216; and Robert I. Crane, "Technique and Method in Social History," in O. P. Bhatnagar, ed., *Studies in Social History (Modern India)* (Allahabad, 1964), 1–21.

at least in certain sectors of life and of the economy. This change—uneven and at times paradoxical—calls for careful analysis and evaluation. So far the explication of change, development, and modernization in South Asia has been fragmentary and inadequate, for the roots of many changes go back to the nineteenth century and the historical dimensions have not been properly examined.[25] Too much of the material in print is purely descriptive and concerned with isolated aspects of modernizing changes.

For example, one significant question for which historical background is required is the extent to which and the ways in which modernization and economic development have changed the traditional caste system of classes and class relationships. Observers disagree over what is happening to caste as classes emerge from the archaic caste system.[26] This intricate question, for which we do not as yet have sufficient, relevant factual information, is further complicated by the fact that India is still predominantly an agrarian society in which more than fifty per cent of the gross national product comes from agriculture and upwards of seventy per cent of the gainfully employed are in the agrarian sector. Not only are the data on the agrarian sector relatively inadequate, but agrarian and land-tenure relationships are murky, imprecise, and difficult to grasp, because attempts at "land reform" in the several Indian states have led to various local efforts to avoid or to mitigate changes.

This is, however, an old problem. Land tenure and landed relationships have been crucial to the control and allocation of

[25] See, for example, the important controversy over economic trends in nineteenth-century India and the fate of the various handicraft industries. A sound grasp of such trends is essential as groundwork to any calculations regarding the condition and starting point from which modernization and development of the Indian economy after the opening of the Suez Canal had to take place. The controversy in question is between Morris D. Morris and his critics. See Morris D. Morris, "Towards a Reinterpretation of Nineteenth Century Indian Economic History," *Indian Economic and Social History Review*, 5 (1968): 1–15; Robert I. Crane, "Technical Education and Economic Development in India before World War I," in C. A. Anderson and M. J. Bowman, eds., *Education and Economic Development* (Chicago, 1963), 167–201; and the review by André Betaille of Lloyd Rudolph and Susann Rudolph, *The Modernity of Tradition: Political Development in India* (Chicago, 1968), in *Indian Economic and Social History Review*, 7 (1970): 417–26.

[26] F. G. Bailey, *Caste and the Economic Frontier* (Manchester, 1960); André Betaille, *Caste, Old and New* (Bombay, 1969); F. G. Bailey, *Tribe, Caste and Nation* (Manchester, 1960).

power in India since the beginnings of recorded history and have caused many vexations for European administrators and historians since British rule commenced. European concepts of land tenure are substantially different from traditional Indian concepts of landholding and landed relationships.[27] In the Indian setting the crucial issue in landholding seems normally to have been the control and management of people. The control of arable land means the control of people, at the least as clients, for by means of the right to dispose of customary shares of what was produced, resources and people were controlled. Shares of produce and other aspects of control of production in the land could be hypothecated, purchased, or even inherited—though certain kinds of collectivities often held rights to land jointly. But land as such could not be bought or sold, partly because of shared interests in its product, so that no individual and no single family could hold indisputable title to the soil.

When the English East India Company imposed its interpretation of Indian tenurial arrangements, modified somewhat to suit the company's needs, upon the districts the company had acquired, it meant a revolution in Indian agrarian systems.[28] The engrafting of alien, European concepts of property and land law onto the Indian systems of landed relations resulted in hybrid systems—different also in various parts of British India because the company tried different tenurial experiments in each great region—that tended to proliferate as long as they paid suitable "revenues," or land taxes, into the coffers of the government of India at a reasonable cost of collection.[29]

Generally speaking, the government collected the revenue or

[27] See Neale, "Land Is To Rule," and Embree, "Landholding in India and British Institutions."

[28] See the thorough discussion in the well-known *Fifth Report of the Select Committee of the House of Commons,* ed. Walter Firminger (Calcutta, 1918), and Ranjit Guha, *A Rule of Property for Bengal* (Paris, 1963).

[29] For a discussion of the major systems of land-revenue settlement in British India, see Ravinder Kumar, "The Deccan Riots of 1875," *Journal of Asian Studies,* 24 (1965): 613–35; E. I. Brodkin, "Proprietary Mutations and the Mutiny in Rohilkhand," *Journal of Asian Studies,* 28 (1969): 667–83; Nilmani Mukherjee, *The Ryotwari System in Madras, 1792–1827* (Calcutta, 1962); Dietmar Rothermund, "The Record of Rights in British India," *Indian Economic and Social History Review,* 8 (1971): 443–61; and L. Brennan, "Social Change in Rohilkhand, 1801–1833," *Indian Economic and Social History Review,* 7 (1970): 443–65.

land tax from a class of superior holders of one description or another, sometimes entitled zamindars (from *zamin*, meaning "land," and *dar*, meaning "holder"), while the various types or categories of superior holders, in turn, collected rents from intermediaries or from tenants who were normally the actual cultivators of the soil. Even in those parts of British India in which the land-revenue demand had supposedly been "settled" with the actual cultivators, it often turned out that intermediaries—local magnates, heads of kin groups, or moneylenders—interposed themselves between government and cultivator.[30] The result was an incredibly complex set of tenure and intermediary relationships, with a wide variety of legal arrangements governing tenancies and under-tenancies recognized by the British courts. These conditions have obviously considerably confused the questions of class structure and class relations.

If the introduction of European concepts of property and the rule of law laid the groundwork for the process of modernization, the monetization of the Indian economy, which had only partly been achieved before 1757, was the engine of the process and was largely accomplished by the end of the nineteenth century. During the same period railways, highways, steamboats, banks, warehouses, insurance agencies, telegraph lines, printing presses, cotton-ginning and baling devices, jute mills, the penny post, cotton textile mills, newspapers, the modern stock exchange, and power-driven machinery initiated the transformation of the economy and modernization of the production and exchange system, while a growing number of secondary schools and colleges doubled and trebled their output of graduates.[31] By the beginning of the

[30] For a discussion of the ways in which moneylenders, for example, could supravene between cultivator and revenue collector, see Prakash Tandon, *Punjabi Century, 1857–1947* (Lahore, 1961); S. S. Thorburn, *Musalmans and Moneylenders in the Punjab* (London, 1886); Kumar, "The Deccan Riots of 1875"; Robert I. Crane, "Strata Disruption and Social Change in South Asia," *United Asia*, 6 (1954): 228–34; and Edward Thornton, *India, Its State and Prospects* (London, 1835).

[31] See Amalendu Guha, "Raw Cotton of Western India," *Indian Economic and Social History Review*, 9 (1972): 1–42; T. A. Timberg, "A North Indian Firm As Seen through Its Business Records, 1860–1914," *Indian Economic and Social History Review*, 8 (1971): 264–83; Ira Klein, "Wilson vs. Trevelyan: Finance and Modernization in India after 1857," *Indian Economic and Social History Review*, 7 (1970): 179–209; B. B. Chaudhuri, "Growth of Commercial Agriculture and Its

twentieth century the crucial questions were who would control the modernization process and in whose benefit would it operate. The Indian nationalist elites were demanding that the levers of power be transferred into their hands, fairly rapidly and more or less completely. Their British rulers, although not of one mind, disagreed over when, if ever, such power could or should be handed to Indians. In addition there was serious disagreement over the terms on which power should be transferred or shared and over the character of the groups in Indian society with whom power ought to be shared. By the end of the nineteenth century these problems had materially affected the interpretation of Indian history and society, as senior British administrators published opinions holding that it would be most difficult to create a meaningful and equitable system of representation for a society divided into so many separate communities, sects, castes, tribes, and interests. From this it logically followed that power could not properly be transferred to Indian hands because no arrangement could be devised that would produce a truly representative body. The corollary seemed to be that the British bureaucracy, which ruled in the interests of all of the people, must continue to hold power. These considerations gave a powerful thrust to the British emphasis upon the significance of sects, castes, and interests as separate electoral groupings in modern Indian society. In this sense, at the least, present politics brought forth its own version of history.

A part of the concern with divisions in society, which would minimize the possibility of devising a suitable, equitable, or effective electoral system in British India, was the post-Mutiny British obsession with the so-called martial races. The mutiny in the sepoy army ("sepoy" is the Persian term for "soldier" and was applied to native troops in India) had led to a great deal of introspection concerning army and recruitment policy. A body of

---

Impact on the Peasant Economy," *Indian Economic and Social History Review*, 7 (1970): 211–51; B. B. Chaudhuri, "Growth of Commercial Agriculture in Bengal, 1859–1885," *Indian Economic and Social History Review*, 7 (1970): 25–60; Blair Kling, "The Origin of the Managing Agency System in India," *Journal of Asian Studies*, 26 (1966): 37–48; R. S. Rungta, *Rise of Business Corporations in India, 1851–1900* (Cambridge, 1970); and Daniel Thorner, "Emergence of an Indian Economy, 1760–1960," *The Encyclopedia Americana* (1960), vol. 15.

doctrine had grown up—much of it based on impressions, half-truths, and stereotypes—that labeled certain communities as "loyal" and "martial" and others as "disloyal," "incompetent," or "cowardly." As in much of this sort of generalization, rigor of observation and empirical evidence were notoriously absent. Widely different types of groups were blithely lumped together under the same rubric, and vast congeries, such as "all Bengalis" or "all Pathans," were consigned en masse to one camp or the other. From this time forward recruitment to the Indian army was to be limited solely to the martial races, whose sturdy reliability and bluff loyalty were stressed in legend, history, and song.

From what has been discussed, the reader may gain a feeling for the kinds of imperatives that influenced the writing of India's history in the century prior to the winning of independence. In large part these biases were serious because they became part of the environment, normally not questioned, let alone challenged. When they were challenged it was usually in polemic terms, on the basis of a contrary faith and a competing rhetoric. The problem of the past two decades has been to rescue South Asian history from the contending sets of shibboleths. New data, provisional understandings, and fresh interpretations have now begun to emerge. The balance of this essay will attempt a summary sketch of the new literature and the highlights of the emerging historical view.

Prehistory

The earliest evidences of human habitation in South Asia can now be dated back to approximately 200,000 B.C., from which era stone implements have been recovered. Neolithic remains, burials, and hearths dating from 6000–5000 B.C. have been uncovered by several archeological digs. But the bulk of the evidence exposed by archeology deals with the Harappan culture of the Indus River valley, parts of Sind, the Punjab plain, regions of Rajasthan and Kathiawar. Elements of Harappan material culture have been uncovered in the remains of villages that dotted these regions, as well as sites in the Persian Gulf, where the active commerce of Mohenjodaro and Harappa clearly went.[32]

For reasons that are unclear the impressive culture of the cities of Mohenjodaro and Harappa declined about 1500 B.C. Sometime thereafter they were covered by desert sands. Thereupon less-civilized peoples came to predominate in North India. These peoples occupied stages in the transition between hunting-gathering and settled agriculture. They used stone tools and copper implements and manufactured an ochre-colored pottery. They seem to have occupied much of North India when the Indo-Aryan-speaking peoples invaded the subcontinent from the northwest around 1100 B.C.

Apparently painted gray ware was associated with the Indo-Aryans; their sites have been found across North India and date from 800 to 500 B.C. Iron dating back to about 800 B.C. has been found at a number of these sites. The sites also show that the horse and cattle had been domesticated and agriculture developed on a systematic basis.

By 500 B.C. the superior technology of the Ganges Valley had made its way into the Deccan Plateau of South India along with iron tools and a refined black, polished pottery. The southward movement of the Indo-Aryan speakers can be traced by noting the location of iron tools, weapons, and polished black ware.

In the south the local Megalithic culture area was noted for its fine black and red pottery as well as for the use of tanks built to store water for cultivation. The latter suggests considerable cooperative effort and centralized direction of labor, for these tanks were by no means small. The peoples involved in the various cultures and sites so far mentioned included Negritos, Proto-Australoids, Mongoloids, Mediterraneans, western Brachycephals, and Nordics.

The Vedic Period

The Indo-Aryan folk entered from the Caspian region, probably as part of a widespread folk movement spread over a century or more and involving the slow but steady

[32] For recent studies of the Harappan culture and of the two great cities, see Romilla Thapar, *A History of India*, 1 (Baltimore, 1966), and K. A. Nilakanta Sastri, *Advanced History of India* (Bombay, 1970), 20–30.

migration of a number of tribes and war bands seeking fertile plains for pastures. When they came to India they were primarily a pastoral, cattle-breeding people. As they settled in North India they became acculturated to the peasant village dwellers they found there, and pastoralism slowly gave way to agriculture.

The Aryan literature indicates that the Indo-Aryans looked down upon the darker-colored people they found in India, whom they apparently had to conquer, and the Vedic hymns are studded with derogatory epithets and mutterings against their enemies, whom they slew with pleasure and robbed with joy. But the Indo-Aryans also borrowed ideas, cultural practices, and women from those whom they enslaved. At that time the plain was forested, and settlements had to be carved out with hard work. The royal virtues of warfare, hunting, and protection could thrive in that environment.

The Indo-Aryans lived in clans or federations of clans, each of which had a king, though there were a few governed by an oligarchy based upon a type of semipopular assembly. These have been described as republican. Because the Indo-Aryans were pastoralists, nature was an ever-present and, at times, threatening reality; their hymns to the gods reflect their reverence for nature and their fear of its hostile aspects. Vedic cult practices and sacrificial rituals were largely concerned with propitiation of the various deities.[33] The sacrifices were accompanied by the chanting of Vedic hymns. The absolutely correct chanting of the relevant hymns was an essential part of the sacrificial formula. Errors in recitation could vitiate the performance and draw the wrath of the gods. This concern over the precision of the chants and the need to commit them to memory led to the development of systematic grammar and lexical rules. Panini, presumably the first great grammarian, was a Brahman whose career was devoted to the systematic analysis of language. The Brahmans, who composed the rituals and the hymns and who alone knew the intricate sacrificial

[33] On the Vedic age and its distinctive ethos, see J. A. B. van Buitenen, "Vedic and Upanisadic Bases of Indian Civilization," in J. W. Elder, ed., *Chapters in Indian Civilization* (Dubuque, 1970), 1: 1–38; Nilakanta Sastri, *Advanced History of India*, 35–63; Thapar, *History of India*, 1: 37–49; Basham, *The Wonder That Was India*, *passim*; and William T. de Bary, ed., *Sources of Indian Tradition* (New York, 1958), *passim*.

formulas, came to occupy a very special place in Vedic society. The special potency of their sacred rites caused them to be called the "god compellers": their chants, if correctly performed, could compel the gods to grant the boons men sought.

Most scholars agree that the mingling of Vedic ideas and practices with those of the indigenous peoples created the highly complex but dynamic basis for the evolution of Hindu society and culture.[34] This evolution can be seen in part in the Upanishads, treatises in prose and verse that reflect striking changes in attitude in the post-Vedic era.

Vedic society was composed of three major classes, or varna. First among these were the Brahmans, who were the priests, intellectuals, astrologers, and ritual specialists. On the basis of their hieratic specialization, various Brahman castes separated off, adopted distinctive caste names, endogamous rules, and gildlike characteristics. At that time, however, the caste system retained flexibility, merit still playing a prominent role along with skill in one's calling. Each major family or clan of Brahmans tended to guard as a valued treasure its rare copies of a recension of one of the Vedas or of the many commentaries thereon. These sacred texts came to be off limits to the uninitiated (i.e., non-Brahmans), especially in the period after the death in 240 B.C. of the Mauryan emperor Ashoka.

The second major class in Vedic society, the Kshatriyas, was that of the rulers, administrators, and warriors. In Vedic times this class was open to men of ability and vigor who distinguished themselves as warriors or able governors. On a number of occasions low-caste kings violently seized a throne. One could always locate an ambitious or hungry Brahman genealogist who, for a consideration, could refurbish a family tree. There developed between rulers and Brahmans an important symbiotic relationship founded on the need of the rulers for sacerdotal legitimation by means of the appropriate sacrifices. The Brahmans, in turn, depended upon lucrative court appointments and the support given by rulers and magnates to the temples and the corporations of Brahmans managing them. In addition rulers granted settled

---

[34] See the excellent account in J. F. Staal, "Sanskrit and Sanskritization."

agricultural villages to Brahman families as a form of benefice, and the bulk of the economic surplus of such Brahman-dominated villages went to support the Brahmans.[35]

The third class, or category, of Vedic society included all of the ritually pure, respectable occupations or castes and was known as the Vaisya. Specialization and gild traits soon created a number of endogamous Vaisya castes, each with its distinctive way of life, preferred occupation, and its own rules governing ritual purity and social contact or intercourse.

Beneath the three respectable orders of Vedic society was the substratum of Sudras, or "menials," who served in ritually unclean capacities and lowly tasks. The indigenous population that had been conquered by the Indo-Aryans were destined to hold the position of Sudras.

The force of caste as a form of social organization has been so great that over the centuries society has been repeatedly bifurcated into larger and larger numbers of separate social compartments, known in India as jati, each of which is endogamous and has its own distinctive customs and regulations governing social distance. In this context it is interesting to note the extent to which minor peculiarities in life-style or occupation have, over time, come to denote separate endogamous castes. In a land in which transport and communications were, until a hundred years ago, difficult and time consuming, the effective terrestrial span covered by the marriage network of each caste was probably never more than a radius of fifty or sixty miles.

Classical Hindu Society

As settled village agriculture became the dominant pursuit in Hindu India, there took place the proliferation of the characteristic set of village artisans who were numbered among the clean, Vaisya castes and the menial Sudra castes. The village, the major unit of social and economic life, tended to manage its own intramural affairs with a minimum of

---

[35] See Burton Stein, "Economic Functions of a Medieval South Indian Temple," *Journal of Asian Studies*, 19 (1960): 163–76; and Stein, "Coromandel Trade in Medieval India," 47–62.

interference from outside. It should not, however, be supposed either that the village was self-sufficient or that it was not in certain respects part of a larger integrative system, though it is clear that the larger integrative systems into which villages could be drawn varied widely in their scope, character, structure, and degree of organization over the face of the Indian land mass.[36]

Self-sufficiency was limited by the extent to which each locality produced the necessary raw materials, apart from foodstuffs. Regional or interregional trade, carried by itinerant merchants, supplied the villages with raw materials required by village artisans but not locally available. When crops failed, food grains had to be brought in or the village folk had to wander and forage. Most villages were exogamous, so that brides had to be recruited from other villages in the region. Market towns and periodic fairs served the intraregional exchange needs of clusters of villages.

The varieties of large integrative systems, often multilevel, have been described, as a general type, as territorially segmented units in which the political boundaries are largely coterminous with those of significant social relationships such as marriage, caste, and exchange. Of one such case Professor Stein has remarked:

> These nuclear areas [of settled, village-based agriculture] were integrated in administration, particularly during periods of important political and military consolidation, as under the imperial Cholas; ... religiously, through numerous settlements of Brahmans, the priestly elite, and through the Hindu temples; and socially and economically through caste groups and caste assemblies. . . . Finally, integration was achieved through the activities of merchant organizations and trade.[37]

Warrior notables, magnates, governors, and viceroys, as well as kings and self-styled chakravartins, or emperors, in turn provided their own varieties and degrees of integration. Kingship was probably the most common political institution throughout the long period of Hindu history. From Vedic times the king, through

---

[36] See Stein, "Coromandel Trade in Medieval India"; Stein, "Brahman and Peasant in Early South Indian History"; Tapan Raychaudhuri, "Permanent Settlement in Operation: Bakarganj District," in Frykenberg, *Land Control and Social Structure in Indian History*, 163–74; and Kumar, *Western India in the Nineteenth Century*, 1–42.
[37] Stein, "Coromandel Trade in Medieval India," 53.

the special ministrations of the priests, was thought to be imbued with quasi-divine attributes, though the villages may have sent elders to assist the ruler in a sabha, or council. Normally there developed around the king and court a bureaucratic entourage of clerks, scribes, stewards, and land-revenue officials. Given the semidivine status of the anointed ruler, his special powers to protect society and bless the harvests, the king could lay claim to a share of the produce of all cultivated lands, a portion of trade profits, and a substantial share of mineral wealth from his domain. A variety of other taxes were also levied by royal officials.[38]

The family was the basic unit of classical Hindu society and was organized on a patriarchal and patrilocal basis in most parts of the subcontinent. The family was, however, embedded in lineage and allied systems of kinship and in its natal caste. In classical times it is supposed that the typical Hindu family was normally the joint or extended family of two or more generations residing at one common homesite, of which all the male offspring and unmarried daughters were members. Daughters married into the home of their husband. The typical Hindu home was normally an all-inclusive building, sheltering the extended family and their domestic animals.

In this sedentary context custom largely occupied the place of law, and the Brahmans acted as coadjutors to the various respectable castes vis-à-vis their customary norms. The king and his purohit, or chief Brahman adviser, were the supreme or final arbiters, the guardians of the customary law, and the regulators of caste.

Magadha, under King Bimbasara, came to dominate what we know as Bihar in the second half of the sixth century B.C. and by conquest and clever marriage alliances took control of the trade routes to the seaports of the Ganges Delta. Bimbasara built roads to facilitate defense and the collection of taxes, but these roads also assisted trade, and the merchant gilds grew in wealth and influence. Bimbasara probably adopted the policies that the Hindu ruler was entitled to one-sixth of the gross produce of all

---

[38] See the excellent discussion of archaic Hindu economic thought and practice in J. J. Spengler, *Indian Economic Thought* (Durham, 1971).

cultivated land as a royal tax and that all open and uncultivated land was Crown land. Royal sanction was therefore required for the opening of new land to cultivation. In 493 B.C. his son Ajatasatru took the throne and embarked on an ambitious campaign of annexation in the Ganges Plain. Soon thereafter a usurper of low social origin occupied the throne of Magadha and became the first Nanda dynast. He resumed the campaign of imperial aggrandizement, financing his wars by a highly systematized collection of the land tax and the creation of a canal network that carried the waters of the Ganges outward to irrigate a broad area. In 321 B.C. Chandragupta Maurya in turn usurped the Nanda throne and developed to its highest potential an irrigated, agrarian-based, intensively systematized, and regulated imperial rule, built upon the Magadhan origins of Bimbasara.[39]

Meanwhile as early as 530 B.C. a Persian satrapy had been created in northwest India at Gandhara, facilitating trade and cultural exchange between North India, Persia, and Greece. As one consequence, in 327 B.C. Alexander, who had conquered Persia, marched into Gandhara and across the Punjab. Though his army withdrew, Greek outposts and satrapies were left behind in the Indus region, and contacts between India and Greek civilization increased.

The capture of power by Chandragupta Maurya signaled the emergence of a new imperial hegemony across North India. The Mauryan kingdom was marked by a greater degree of political and administration integration than any of its predecessors. In 297 B.C. Chandragupta was succeeded by his son, Bindusara, who pushed Mauryan hegemony into the Deccan Plateau, as far south as Mysore. When he died in 272 B.C. about seventy-five per cent of the subcontinent was under Mauryan domination. Bindusara's son, the Emperor Ashoka, finally conquered Kalinga, the last great province.

Fortunately Ashoka (272–240 B.C.) erected a series of pillars on which were cut edicts, inscriptions, and grants, and from these

---

[39] It was the Mauryan kingdom that produced the *Arthasastra,* the ultimate in the doctrine of statecraft from a Hindu source. Kautilya, presumed to have been Chandragupta's chief minister, was the author. The *Arthasastra* portrays a highly regulated, rationalized, and codified state in which the lives of the citizens were governed for the well-being of the kingdom. For a good discussion of the *Arthasastra,* see Spengler, *Indian Economic Thought,* 50–82.

we get much of our knowledge of the emperor and of his kingdom. As is well known, soon after he conquered Kalinga he was converted to Buddhism and renounced wars of aggression. In 250 B.C. the third Buddhist world council convened at his capital, Pataliputra.

By this time land revenue had come to be the backbone of imperial revenues, and the administration was primarily concerned with the efficient collection of land tax, though a variety of other taxes were also collected. In addition the Ashokan kingdom organized the opening of new land as a branch of state activity and used Sudras as *corvée* labor. Irrigation works were developed and maintained by the state, and irrigation waters were distributed under a system of charges. In addition the Mauryan kingdom employed shipbuilders, armorers, stone masons, and sculptors. Through gifts the state enabled the great temples to employ many craftsmen in construction.

The urban gilds of artisans, bankers, and merchants seem to have grown powerful in Ashokan times and appear to have largely controlled urban affairs, though their Vaisya caste status would deny to them the ritual and class position that should have accompanied their economic power. Perhaps as a measure of resentment against Brahman support for the caste system, which militated against their status claims, many merchants became Buddhists or Jains, members of non-Brahman sects.

Ashoka's kingdom was divided into four major provinces, each governed by a royal prince as viceroy. There were also subordinate units under local governors, most of whom were local magnates who had accepted Mauryan hegemony. The emperor sent his officials out on tours to inspect the activities of the governors and employed a variety of spies to report on all public officials. The districts were subdivided into circles, groups of villages called pergunnahs, and each pergunnah had an accountant–record keeper as well as a chief revenue collector. The two acted as a check upon each other, though both cooperated to levy and collect land and other taxes and to keep all relevant records. This system of local administration was handed down, largely unchanged, from Mauryan to Mughal times and in turn, further modified, bequeathed to the British.

Within this context of administrative integration each village developed an internal integration based, at least in North India, on the jajmani system of interdependent patron-client relations. The upper castes were the jajmans (patrons), who utilized the artisan or labor skills of the kamins (clients) in the lower castes. Remuneration for service was customary, partly noneconomic, hierarchically graded, and asymmetrical. The kamin was not reimbursed for the amount or quality of his product; he was a retainer and received customary boons.[40]

After the collapse of the Mauryan dynasty in 185 B.C., political trends in most of India were chaotic. Kings, claimants, and magnates, as well as invaders from central Asia, vied for hegemony or hacked out local domains. Usurpations, wars, and Scythian tribal attacks marked the age. While the Kushanas were building a dynasty in the area between Peshawar and Mathura, about A.D. 80, the Satavahana dynasty, controlling the Godaveri Valley, had climbed to eminence in the northern Deccan. This dynasty, strong supporters of the Brahmans, maintained close contacts with North India, kept cultural avenues open, and facilitated the spread of Sanskritic texts to the south.

During the early centuries of the Christian era the Chola kings in South India consolidated their power and gained virtual supremacy over the peninsula. Because they controlled the important overland routes between the coastal seaports, the Chola rulers were in a strategic position vis-à-vis the interocean trade and carried on a valuable trade with Rome. By the fourth century A.D. India was crossed by intersecting trade routes, some of which had seaport terminals, while others fed trans-Indian trade networks into central and western Asia. Trade, the movement of ideas and technology, and the accumulations of wealth made possible new adaptations to the environment, new social and economic configurations, and new levels of integration.

In this it is possible to discern, at least in South India, the development of levels of integration, each with its own distinctive organizational attributes and allocation of authority over resources. Professor Stein speaks of such integration as an agrarian system, which he characterizes as a set of relations between

[40] For additional information on the jajmani system, see T. O. Biedelman, *A Comparative Analysis of the Jajmani System* (New York, 1959).

"people, groups of people, and the land as a systemic unity, a whole."[41] Stein posits one of the great institutions in the eleventh century A.D. to have been the merchant association, which ranged over the entire southern portion of the peninsula and had towns and villages as marts under its control. There was, at the same time, a special type of territorial assembly, the chitrameliperiyanedu. These assemblies were controlled by agriculturists and dominated the affairs of densely cultivated areas of settled agriculture, which provided the consumers for the trade carried by the merchant gilds.

But in the fourteenth century the peasant assemblies vanished because of changes in the agrarian system of the south, and with their collapse the great merchant gilds, dependent upon a symbiotic relationship, soon disappeared. In place of the peasant assemblies arose a new kind of integration based upon warrior control. Raids and attacks into the Chola kingdom by hostile forces across the borders led to new types of defensive arrangements in the Chola heartland, arrangements favoring the rise of a new regional warrior elite. This elite created for itself a quasi-autonomous position with regard to the Chola overlord, who became a nominal and tributary superior. Because the new warrior elite was recruited from a variety of sources, there was no tradition of loyalty to the class or to the overlord, and hence there were no institutions making for cohesion around a centralizing power. Loyalties, that is to say, were distinctively parochial, with the warrior elite integrating their private jurisdictions by eliminating pre-existing corporate bodies. Moreover the prominent warrior nobles now directly managed agrarian resources, reduced the autonomy of Brahman villages, and abolished the autonomy of associations such as gilds.

In the meantime, after the period of chaos already mentioned, there had emerged in A.D. 319 in North India the new Gupta empire, which seems to have resembled the later phase of the tributary overlordship of the Cholas in the south. In the north the several existing jurisdictions under local warrior rulers owed nominal loyalty and payment of tribute to the Gupta ruler. In

---

[41] Stein, "Integration of the Agrarian System of South India."

its artistic, cultural, and intellectual activity, however, the Gupta court can properly claim classical status. Chandra Gupta II, who reigned from A.D. 375 to 415, carried the cultural standards of the dynasty to their highest level. Kalidasa, the pre-eminent Sanskrit poet, was a member of his court. Literary remains and evidence from excavations make it obvious that during the two centuries following Chandra Gupta's reign the standard of living for the more affluent classes was high and articles of luxury were by no means rare.[42]

At this time Indian knowledge of metals and metallurgy was already highly advanced. The iron pillar of Delhi, dating from approximately this era, was cast in one piece twenty-three feet high, and in more than one thousand years it has scarcely rusted. In the same period a life-size standing copper Buddha was cast in two parts. Coins were finely struck, and dies carefully engraved. The seals attached to the many copper-plate inscriptions, bestowing royal grants, were also of high quality. The same age was one of vigorous development of Indian mathematics. By the fifth century the decimal system and the zero were in regular use among Indian mathematicians, and at a later date Indian numerals were introduced to the world by the Arabs as Arabic numerals.

The Age of Muslim Hegemony

Early in the eighth century A.D. Arabs secured a foothold in a corner of Sind and began to carve out petty principalities. The important Hindu kingdoms of North India, unaware of the Islamic power and civilization of the Middle East, paid little attention to these Muslim newcomers. A Turkish army sacked and looted Kanauj in A.D. 1018 and thus broke the power of an important North Indian state for the first time. But the various dynasties in North India, led by Hindu rulers, called Rajputs, of Hindu clans, continued their internecine rivalries, perpetuating those conditions of antagonism that invited outsiders to intervene. The Rajputs prided themselves on their chivalric code and their willingness to die on the field of battle rather than surrender. Fierce clan rivalry kept the Rajputs hostile to

---

[42] Thapar, *History of India*, 1: 151.

each other and prevented them from uniting in defense of nationality or religion.

Between 1008 and 1026 Mahmud of Ghazni, in Afghanistan, invaded North India more than once, seizing and looting the major holy centers of Mathura, Thanesar, Kanauj, and Somnath. The temples of Somnath had icons and fittings of immense value, many in solid gold. But Mahmud's raids still did not alert the rulers of India to the menace just across the border. By 1182 Mohammed of Ghor had brought all of Sind under his suzerainty. In 1185 he conquered Lahore, in the Punjab, and began to attack the various Rajput kingdoms that stood between him and the mid-Ganges Plain. In 1192 at the second battle of Tarain he bested the Rajput armies and took the kingdom of Delhi. From that time forward, one Muslim ruler or another occupied the throne at Delhi, a strategically significant position. With the Delhi kingdom as the heartland of an empire, the Muslims could extend control in several directions, collecting land revenues on heavily cultivated areas and controlling the major trade routes of the Ganges Plain. Positioned at Delhi, Muslim power was in an excellent location to spread its sway across Hindustan.

Islam modified Indian society in several different ways, though by no means uniformly or rapidly. Many strands of Islam came into India, not only different ethnic groups bearing the Muslim faith but also major differences in doctrine, for there were Shias, Sunnis, Sufis, and followers of other schools of Islamic thought. Some of these, such as the mystics of various persuasions, mingled with bhakti and other Hindu cults to form new, synthetic Indo-Muslim spiritual groups.

Similarly Muslim style and principles merged with Hindu traditions in a new blend of Indo-Saracenic architecture and art—as, for example, in the celebrated miniatures of the Rajasthani school. There also developed a new hybrid language of the camp and market—Hindustani—with a mixed Persian and Hindi vocabulary. The literary version of this language, Persian-Urdu, used the Arabic script and the hybrid vocabulary of Hindustani. Poetry and prose of refined taste flourished in Persian-Urdu, and it came to be the court language of the Muslim rulers and administrators.

By and large Muslim rulers superimposed their administrations upon existing Hindu magnates, whose administrative and revenue systems were often more sophisticated and better suited to local circumstances than those imported by the invading Muslims. It was normally easier to employ experienced local administrators who had close contact with the local population than to use alien officials. As a result there was not much transformation of the system by the Muslim take-over. In addition the Muslim conquerors came from agrarian-based societies not too dissimilar from those of India, so that their systems of government would not have been substantially different in any event.

Some of the Muslim rulers were iconoclasts and destroyers of temples, but many allowed their non-Muslim subjects to pursue their religion in peace and molested them in no way, except perhaps to collect the jiziya, or poll tax upon non-Muslims. The sultans largely followed the basic law of Islam, the Sharia, as interpreted by the ulema, a body of learned Muslim theologians. The ruler was advised directly by the chief qazi, or high judge, though the sultan was often himself the final authority, under the Holy Koran. In theory the Muslim ruler in India was a representative of the caliph of Islam, though in practice this had limited meaning. Nonetheless, the ultramontane interests of the Muslims stimulated trade and other contacts with western and central Asia, for Indian Islam was part of a larger Islamic world and constant contacts with the Muslim homelands were maintained.[43]

By 1526, when the Mughals arrived in India, a pattern of Indo-Islamic society had developed in which a reasonable degree of accommodation, and at some levels assimilation, had taken place, even though upper-caste Hindus probably resented the political dominance of the Muslims, many of whom were in their eyes of low and unclean status and some of whom were converts from low Hindu castes. To preserve their caste purity, the Brahmans

[43] On Islam in India, see Yusaf Husain, *Glimpses of Medieval Indian Culture* (Bombay, 1957); I. H. Qureslir, *The Muslim Community of the Indo-Pakistan Subcontinent* (New York, 1960); Ibn Batuta, *Ibn Batuta's Travels*, tr. H. A. R. Gibb (London, 1929–62); Abul Fazl, *Akbar Namah*, tr. Henry Beveridge (Calcutta, 1897–1921); N. A. Bakshi, *Tabaqat-i-Akbari*, tr. Barun De (Calcutta, 1927–39); Peter Hardy, *Historians of Medieval India* (London, 1960); R. P. Tripathi, *Rise and Fall of the Mughal Empire* (Allahabad, 1960); Tapan Raychaudhuri, *Bengal under Akbar and Jahangir* (Calcutta, 1953); Irfan Habib, *The Agrarian System of Mughal India* (New York, 1963); Ishwari Prasad, *Life and Times of Humayun* (Bombay, 1956); and Percival Spear, *Twilight of the Mughals* (Cambridge, 1951).

and orthodox high-caste groups turned inward, cultivating ritual and enhancing the rules that controlled social contact and intermingling. At the same time, however, Hindu mystic cults, such as the bhakti cults, were influenced by Islamic mysticism. The rise of Sikhism was, of course, the most overt exemplification of these syncretic tendencies.[44]

The south, meanwhile, was divided along the Krishna River between the Bahmani sultanate, consisting of several Islamic provinces, each seeking virtual autonomy, and the Hindu Vijayanagar kingdom, based upon a number of warrior jurisdictions from which it drew tribute. By 1538 the Bahmani kingdom fell apart, but a few years later the successor states allied against Vijayanagar and managed to defeat it and pillage its magnificent capital city.

When Babur led his Mughal cavalry down from Kabul into the North Indian plain, he found a plethora of warring states. It took him only a short time to win the Delhi kingdom, but he died before Mughal power could be consolidated. His son Humayun was soon driven out of North India and took refuge with the Persian emperor. Eventually the Persian court lent him support, and he marched back to India; en route his son Akbar was born. For the next few years Humayun was fully occupied with the reconquest of the Delhi kingdom. Then he suffered a fatal accident, and in 1565 Akbar came to the throne. During the next forty years he created, consolidated, and disseminated the Mughal Empire, whose chief architect he surely was.

Akbar's first decade on the throne was spent in conquest and pacification, the rest of his remarkable career in the consolidation of the Empire and improvement of its administration. He realized the Mughals were a tiny minority in a vast sea of Hindus and other nationalities. Hence he set himself firmly to create a meritocracy, to be recruited for the service of the state without regard for caste, creed, or national origin. He insisted that religion was a personal affair; tolerance was state policy. He worked hard for reconciliation with the leading Hindu princely houses, concluding marriage alliances with several major Rajput kingdoms and

[44] On Sikhism, see Khushwant Singh, *The Sikhs* (London, 1953); J. C. Archer, *The Sikhs in Relation to Hindus, Moslems, Christians, and Ahmadiyyas* (Princeton, 1946); and M. A. Macauliffe, ed., *Sikh Religion, A Symposium* (Calcutta, 1958).

recruiting these brave warriors as commanders in the imperial army. Meanwhile Hindu scribes and bureaucrats were promoted to upper levels of administration. His chief revenue officer was Todar Mal, a Hindu.[45]

In an effort to centralize the administration and minimize divisive tendencies, Akbar ranked all administrative officers in a graded hierarchy to be centrally hired, fired, and promoted. In addition they were to draw their salary from the imperial treasury, so as to minimize independence or the creation of local bases of power. Each officer supposedly maintained a retinue of troopers, though his official duties might bear no relation to his rank as an officer of men-at-arms. The emperor had the power to assign or transfer any officer to any post or any district at any time. This system, as it was not hereditary, has been described as an official nobility. The rank and title were extinguished at the demotion or death of the holder, and his property was resumed by the state.

The Empire was divided into a number of provinces, each of which was governed by a subedar, or governor, and a diwan, or provincial treasurer, who were to act as a check upon each other. The provincial court and administration tended to mirror on a smaller scale the imperial court and establishment. Each province was, in turn, divided into sarkars, or districts. In the district there was a military officer responsible for defense and law and order and a revenue officer responsible for the levy and collection of imperial and provincial taxes, chief among which was the imperial land-revenue tax. For revenue purposes each district was divided into revenue assessment circles, the pergunnahs. In addition to the basic land tax—a share or portion of production—there were excise taxes, market taxes, duties on certain goods, a salt monopoly, an opium monopoly, and other forms of taxation.

Diwan Todar Mal reformed and reorganized the land-revenue assessment system to arrive at an equitable, average portion of

---

[45] On Mughal administration and Akbar's policies, see A. L. Srivastara, *A Short History of Akbar* (Agra, 1957); Zahir-ud-din Faruki, *Aurangzeb and His Times* (Bombay, 1935); S. M. Ikram, *Muslim Civilization in India* (New York, 1964); Abul Fazl, *Ain-e-Akbari*, tr. K. H. Blochmann (Delhi, 1965); and Philip Calkins, "The Formation of a Regionally Oriented Ruling Group in Bengal, 1700–1740," *Journal of Asian Studies*, 29 (1970): 799–806. Ainslie Embree, ed., *Alberuni's India* (New York, 1971), provides an excellent background to Muslim rule.

typical production from various classes of land, but his system required an elaborate cadastral survey and could not be carried out beyond the confines of the Delhi kingdom proper. In the rest of the Empire rather more rule-of-thumb methods of estimating yields and percentages for collection continued in use.

Increasingly, however, revenue-collection officials and tax farmers—taluqdars, zamindars, and jagirdars—intruded upon the scene, collecting taxes on behalf of the Empire and "reimbursing" themselves for so doing by retaining a percentage of the revenue they collected.[46] Officers who had been salaried, that is to say, began to collect their "salaries" in the form of assignments on the revenues, which is what Akbar's policy had been designed to avoid. A host of evils and oppressions of the cultivators followed. Moreover, as Mughal power fluctuated and power relations shifted, the significance of landed relationships changed in a fluid and kaleidoscopic manner, so that tenancies, estates, holdings, and titles came to have very complex and variegated nomenclatures and meanings.

Essentially, however, the imperial system and the imperial officials sought to centralize administration and revenue affairs as much as possible, while local magnates, underholders, gilds, and village heads tended to exercise as much *de facto* autonomy as they could get away with. As the power of the emperor and the imperial system declined, especially after 1700, the dynamic balance between centralizing imperial power and centrifugal localistic centers of authority shifted. The imperial authorities were forced to strike a bargain with local elites in exchange for revenue and support. The cost was greater autonomy for local magnates and a concomitant transformation of tax farmers into an estate-holding gentry. Moneylenders, or mahajans, who had advanced funds to zamindars and taluqdars, were also able, as the balance shifted, to elbow their way into the circle of estate and power holders.

It should be noted that Akbar's policy of a meritocracy suffered.

[46] On Mughal revenue collectors and tax farmers, see Habib, *Agrarian System of Mughal India;* Neale, "Land Is To Rule"; and S. Nurul Hasan, "Zamindars under the Mughals," in Frykenberg, *Land Control and Social Structure in Indian History*, 17–32. Please note that in a number of cases the Mughals bowed to expediency and appointed as tax farmers those who were already firmly established as local magnates.

Posts tended to become family perquisites, the great zamindars and jagirdars were not easily removed or transferred, and Aurangzeb, the last of the great Mughals, reintroduced certain measures that discriminated in favor of Muslims. When Aurangzeb died in 1707 the grandeur and vigor of the Empire died with him, and the administrative policy, upon which Akbar had based its stability, had been vitiated. The intervening period had, however, witnessed a flowering of important syncretic developments in art, architecture, literature, and belles-lettres. Hindustani had flourished as a new lingua franca, and, especially in court circles and the administrative towns, a mixed culture had emerged, combining the best of Persian and cultured Hindu life-styles.

Unlike the other alien peoples who had entered the subcontinent in previous centuries, the Muslims could not be largely assimilated into the dominant, majority Hindu society. Islam as a codified religion and way of life was sufficiently distinctive, so that the Muslims could remain largely separate from Hindu society. In fact Hinduism reacted by drawing in upon itself, tightening its ranks, and increasing its emphasis upon orthodoxy and exclusiveness.

By 1707, however, a dramatic new element had entered upon the scene, contributing to significant changes in the balance of forces. Within a few years after Aurangzeb's death the Indian Ocean and the coastline had come substantially under European naval power, and that was a major change in the strategic situation of the subcontinent.

The Coming of the Europeans

The Europeans came to Asia in search of overseas sources of commodities and riches such as spices, precious metals, brocades, and porcelain. Improved technology and advanced sailing techniques greatly facilitated the ability of the European maritime powers to navigate the oceans, while the *reconquista* led Iberian powers to strive for decisive victory over Islam.[47] Access to Asian riches was through the Middle East and

---

[47] J. H. Parry, *Europe and a Wider World* (London, 1954), *passim;* Ludovico Varthema, *Travels* (London, 1863); Francois Bernier, *Travels in the Moghul Empire* (London, 1934); E. F. Oaten, *European Travellers in India during the 15th, 16th and 17th Centuries* (London, 1909).

so at the mercy of Arab merchants in Baghdad and Aleppo. The Venetians managed to secure some trading rights in the entrepôt towns of the Middle East, so that other European nations had to depend upon the dual monopoly of the Arabs and the Venetians who transshipped goods back to Europe.

After the capture of Ceuta in 1419, Prince Henry the Navigator set out to create the mechanisms and know-how by which Portugal could break the monopoly and go directly to the sources of supply. By 1498 it was possible for Vasco da Gama to undertake the epoch-making voyage around the tip of Africa, past Madagascar, and across to the Malabar Coast of India. This opened a new age in world history and in the history of the Indian subcontinent. Direct oceanic contact and interchange with Asia involved Europeans with densely populated lands, antique civilizations, highly literate and diversified cultures, and elaborate religions, philosophies, and value systems. The products and art wares of Asia had an immediate and profound effect upon Europe. The intellectual impact of Asia in Europe was slower but also impressive.[48]

The North European states were not willing to leave the rich Asian trade in Portuguese or Spanish hands and by a variety of means penetrated the monopoly the Iberians erected on the basis of da Gama's voyage. The Portuguese monopoly was based upon control of the crucial sea lanes and the few key entrepôt towns they had seized, such as Goa. Operating from these bases, Portuguese armed vessels sought to interdict all trade and prevent carriage of the commodities in which the Portuguese desired a monopoly. Obviously native merchants and native rulers, who derived part of their revenues from trade or taxes on trade, found these monopolistic policies most vexatious. In order to secure or maintain their monopoly, the Portuguese used diplomacy, bribery, and force or threat of force. But as far as South Asia was concerned, the impact of the Portuguese tended to be confined largely to the coastal littoral and seaport enclaves.[49]

[48] Holden Furber, "Asia and the West As Partners, Before Empire and After," *Journal of Asian Studies*, 28 (1969): 711–21.
[49] Kristoff Glamman, *Dutch Asiatic Trade, 1620–1740* (The Hague, 1958); Tapan Raychaudhuri, "The Dutch in Coromandel, 1605–1690" (D. Phil. thesis, Oxford University, 1957); A. Das Gupta, *Malabar in Asian Trade, 1740–1800* (Cambridge, 1967), *passim.*

The real importance of the Portuguese lies in the system of control and intervention they created, which later European powers, such as the Dutch, adopted and applied to the Indian and Asian trade. This system of control over trade—in commodities to be sent back to Europe in Portuguese vessels—involved diverting all movement of such goods to Portuguese ports and thence in Portuguese vessels and also involved special arrangements by which the Portuguese could buy commodities, such as spices, at very favorable prices, usually below free-market prices. In addition the Portuguese were exempt or virtually exempt from payment of excise dues, harbor and portage charges, wharfage dues, and other imposts and taxes that rival merchants, including native traders, had to pay. Naturally the local prince or magnate would not make such concessions to a European power unless coerced or unless he received some special inducement in return. Trade based upon such privileges and upon monopoly control of sources of supply or of the market system could not be a free and peaceful trade. The Portuguese bequeathed to their successors a system of trade that was in essence based upon demands that were political. This involved the merchants, through diplomacy or the use of force, in interstate rivalries and in the effort to create and sustain monopolies and special trading privileges.

By 1596 Holland and England were ready to challenge the Iberian monopoly. Portugal was overextended, making the Dutch and English take-over easier. The Dutch Company of the Indies, more powerful and better financed than the English East India Company, soon adopted the major elements of the monopoly-control system that the Portuguese had created and applied them systematically to Southeast Asia and the Spice Islands.[50]

The English East India Company, chartered by the Crown in 1600, was much more modest. The charter gave the company valuable monopoly privileges in the Asian trade as against all other Englishmen. The employees of the company were subject to strict regulations and were prohibited from trading on their

[50] Sinnappah Arasaratnam, *Dutch Power in Ceylon, 1658–1687* (Amsterdam, 1958); Das Gupta, *Malabar in Asian Trade;* M. A. Meilink-Roelofsz, *Asian Trade and European Influence in the Indonesian Archipelago* (The Hague, 1962).

own account.[51] The first voyage of the company to India landed in 1607 at Surat, an important entrepôt port of the Mughal Empire. This venture was hampered by the Portuguese, who wanted no European rivals trading there. The English were not prepared to tolerate Portuguese interference, and the English fleet severely damaged the Portuguese ships. The English victory considerably impressed the Mughal governor of Surat, who gave the English company favorable trading facilities and lodgings; the company soon constructed a fortified factory or trading center and warehouse. A few years later, in 1637, the company leased a plot of land for a fortified factory complex, where it built Fort St. George near a tiny fishing village on the Coromandel Coast. At this point a major trading complex developed, ideally located for trade to Southeast Asia and for involvement in the economic life of South India. It came to be known as Madras.

In 1664 the island of Bombay, with its fine harbor, on India's west coast, came to the English Crown as part of the dowry of the Portuguese princess who married King Charles II. The English Crown leased Bombay to the East India Company for £10 and a few peppercorns per year. The company gained a major port and fortified commercial center on the Arabian Sea. By the end of the century the company had purchased the zamindari, or tax-collection rights, to three tiny adjacent hamlets at Kali Ghat on the banks of the muddy Hughli River in Bengal, where they soon built Fort William and the rapidly growing metropolis of Calcutta.

These major trading centers—Bombay, Madras, and Calcutta—gave the East India Company direct commercial access to major economic regions and important handicraft areas of India. Soon after the founding of Calcutta and a painful period of intense competition for the Indian Ocean trade, the company

[51] For life in the early English trading centers in India, see Percival Spear, *The Nabobs* (London, 1963), *passim;* John Burnell, *Bombay in the Days of Queen Anne* (London, 1933); W. W. Hunter, *History of British India*, 1 (London, 1899); Ainslie Embree, *Charles Grant and British Rule in India* (New York, 1962); C. H. Philips, ed., introd. to *The Correspondence of David Scott, Director and Chairman of the East India Company* (London, 1951), vol. 1; S. B. Chaudhuri, "The Problems of Financing East India Company's Investments in Bengal: 1650–1720," *Indian Economic and Social History Review*, 8 (1971): 109–33; and Holden Furber, *John Company at Work* (Cambridge, Mass., 1948).

was reorganized and combined with its principal rival into the new and more powerful United Company. This reorganization was most opportune, because very spirited competition from the new French Company of the Indies, headquartered at Pondicherry near Madras, was soon under way.

Each great presidency town, so-called because it was administered by a president and council of senior merchants, handled all the affairs of the English company in the region. Orders came out from the directors in London, who sent to India each year at least one fleet of East Indiamen, laden with goods it was hoped could be sold in the Indies and with specie (the goods and specie together were known as the "investment"), along with a shopping list of the commodities and items to be bought in Asia for profitable resale in Europe. Prominent on the list were textiles like muslins, calicoes, and brocades. The company also drove a profitable inter-Asian trade in country cloths, which were taken from India to Java or Malaya to exchange for spices or other valued commodities to be sold in Europe. The company discovered that opium from India could be sold readily in various ports in Southeast Asia and at Canton, where it conducted the very profitable tea trade.

The company founded subordinate factories, or trade centers, upcountry from Bombay, Madras, and Calcutta. These feeder stations collected trade goods from the villages and localities, brought them together, and forwarded them to the ports for shipment overseas. It was in these upcountry centers that decisive contacts were made with Indian merchants, middlemen, and artisans.

Normally the company could not send out enough specie to buy the goods it ordered, so there was in India a perpetual search for credit with which to buy. Short-term credit was also required because the fleet arrived at stated intervals, but purchasing had to be done between shipments of specie. Fiscal needs came to be solved, at least partly, by local merchants and middlemen, who advanced funds to the company and acted as commission agents in purchasing for the company. Company officers often had a limited command of native languages, and their knowledge of local markets was small. The commission agent supplied this deficiency. These agents were frequently known as dubashes, meaning "two tongues," since they were fluent in English and in an Indian mother tongue.[52] They were, however, much more than translators: they were commission agents, moneylenders, silent partners, and go-betweens. These positions were potentially rich with patronage and formed the basis of a growing comprador class. These men waxed in importance as their English patrons grew in power and prominence.

Once the goods demanded by London were acquired at an upcountry, or mofussul, factory, they were shipped in local boats, bullock carts, or camel trains down to the nearest presidency town for final checking and lading on the outward voyage. As long as Mughal power reigned supreme and general law and order prevailed, these shipments were safe. There was, however, the vexatious problem of local customs and transit duties charged by local magnates, zamindars, and others. Company officers reported, for example, that some fifty-seven imposts had to be paid on goods shipped from Patna in Bihar down to Calcutta. Each impost was a trifle, but when added up they amounted to more than a nuisance, not to mention the delays and pilferage suffered. So the company engaged in high-level diplomacy to secure duty-free passage of their goods. On several occasions an imperial firman, or order, was acquired, which purported to exempt the company from payment of inland duties on goods en route to a port for overseas shipment. Unfortunately, when Mughal power declined local chieftains, or nawabs, tended to stop honoring these edicts. There was room, moreover, for disagreement over interpretation of the firmans.

The edicts clearly referred to company goods, but company officers were trading on their own account and were passing their goods along with shipments of company goods. This not only robbed the local ruler of dues to which he was entitled but also placed all other merchants at a distinct disadvantage in competition with the company merchants who were trading duty free. Frequent quarrels and fights followed. As long as Mughal power was supreme, these affrays could be settled. After 1707, when Mughal power began its steady decline, local authorities took

[52] See C. S. Srinivasachari, ed., *Ananda Ranga Pillai: The "Pepys" of French India* (Madras, 1940). Pillai was a dubash.

matters increasingly into their own hands. The company became more and more aggrieved that its privileges were being undermined, conveniently forgetting that company officers had often abused those privileges to their own advantage.

The rise of would-be successor states in the vacuum created by the collapse of Mughal power added to turbulence, civil strife, and brigandage. Peaceful trade and the safe convoy of goods across country came to be more uncertain. The company hired armed guards to protect its factories and caravans, leading to the formation of sepoy companies and battalions. Of course all of the European trading organizations adopted these practices, not only the English.

Another source of tension was the competition among several European trading companies for the same commodities and the same special trading privileges. When the French Company of the Indies entered the field, backed by royal capital and royal power, the competition for relatively scarce goods became very keen. Handicraft production was, at least in the short run, rather inelastic, with the result that a rapid increase in demand was not readily translated into increased supply. Worse, each company wanted a monopoly of trade. Keen competition between rival companies led to malpractices and to the use of force in an effort to control the sources of supply. All of these factors caused the companies to become increasingly involved in the internal, political affairs of India. Each company obviously desired to see upon the throne a ruler who would honor company contracts and award it special trading privileges not available to competitors. At the same time, the officers of the companies became embroiled in local political affairs because such involvement could be a very profitable exercise. "Shaking the Pagoda Tree," as it came to be called, was an attractive pursuit for the greedy.

Life in India in the eighteenth century was risky, unhealthy, and at times dangerous. When a young man went out as a clerk on the company's establishment, he started at a very small salary. If he survived cholera, plague, and malaria for twelve years, he could hope to become a senior merchant on a reasonable salary. But he had no hope of a fortune or a comfortable retirement unless he engaged in extralegal private trade, smuggled, or took bribes.

Unlike the English and Dutch companies, the French company was more than fifty per cent state owned and had state officers and royal arms. This gave it the advantage of military and naval power not commanded by the English or the Dutch. It also meant, however, that the Crown could dictate French policy in India in view of French national interests in other parts of the globe. The English company, by contrast, was single-minded in its concern for its India (and China) trade and profits.

The French company actively started overt political involvement and kingmaking in India. In 1739 the shah of Persia sacked Delhi and dealt a tragic blow to the remnants of Mughal prestige and power.[53] After that former subordinates behaved as though they were independent rulers, referring to the emperor only when it suited their purposes to do so. A series of conflicts occurred as rivals fought over succession to one or another throne.

In 1741, when the last nawab appointed by Delhi died and two contenders came forward, a civil war broke out in the Mughal province of the Carnatic. The French company decided to support one of the two rivals, "renting" him an army and lending him a military advisory group of French officers to guide his strategy. With this support the French-backed contender won the Carnatic throne. In return for their aid, the new nawab gave rich presents to the French officers and paid all of the expenses and salaries of the French battalions, which removed the cost of those troops from the budget of the French company. This support, of course, made the nawab a client of the French, kept upon his throne by French troops. The age of imperialism had dawned in India. The grateful nawab also gave the French company special trading privileges. A short time later, in lieu of the payments for French troops, the nawab assigned several districts over to the company to collect all the revenues therefrom to serve as reimbursement for the expenses of the battalions.

The English company was horrified at this turn of events. Its officers feared that their rivals had worked a political revolution in a rich and populous region and would soon exclude English commerce from the province. This revolution, moreover, could provide the French company with territorial revenues, or taxes,

[53] See Spear, *Twilight of the Mughals,* and S. P. Sen, *The French in India* (Calcutta, 1958).

to cover overhead and supplement the profits from trade. Meanwhile the English officials watched in envy while the French officers acquired rich rewards from their close association with the Carnatic court. The dazzling prospects for kingmakers and commanders of palace guards were probably too much to resist.

Amidst councils of alarm Robert Clive, a subordinate officer on the company's Madras establishment, advanced a bold plan to regain the initiative. The frightened council accepted Clive's proposal and gave him command of the local sepoys; he counterattacked in support of the rival contender for the throne. With dash, good tactics, and even better luck, Clive defeated the French and their native ally and placed the English candidate upon the Carnatic throne. The French alliance was undone.

Meanwhile events in Bengal created friction between the English and the nawab. By 1756 mutual suspicions and misunderstandings led to the seige of Fort William by a portion of the nawab's army. When Fort William capitulated, there took place the obscure incident, later blown up as the Black Hole of Calcutta, in which some members of the English garrison died in a badly ventilated storeroom, temporarily used as a prison.[54] Disagreements were patched up, and a treaty of amity was signed, but a few weeks later Clive, determined to gain retribution, arrived by sea from Madras with a sepoy army. Because peace had been established he fell to conspiring with disaffected local notables and bankers, and he suborned a commander in the nawab's army. This led to the battle of Plassey, 1757, in which a small number of British and sepoy troops bested the large army of the nawab of Bengal, whose commander had betrayed him. The nawab fled but was caught and beheaded. Two days later Clive placed the traitor upon the gadi, or throne, of Bengal, making it obvious who had made the new ruler.

This act was followed by a round of rich presents for the English officials. Clive was given about £220,000 as a personal gift, and the company received the zamindari of several rich Bengal districts, while promises were made to pay other debts, real and alleged, of the dead nawab to company officials. The new

[54] See Brijen Gupta, *Sirajuddaullah and the East India Company, 1756–1757* (Leiden, 1962).

nawab promised, moreover, not to collect inland duties on the goods of the company in transit. Under this privilege the company officers could continue to pass their own private trade goods duty free, while all other merchants had to pay a variety of dues.

Regrettably the new nawab found the treasury poorer than had been imagined and was not able to pay all of the debts he had assumed. Hopes deferred turned to bitterness, and it was but natural that a project was formed to install a more compliant man in his place. This was soon accomplished, along with a fresh distribution of gifts and additional zamindari districts to the company, which now began to hope that its costs in India could be met from tax revenues.

The new nawab proved to be an able and hardheaded man. He could not pay his debts to the company unless he collected all the duties and taxes available, a plan that infuriated the officers of the company who were trading duty free. In the controversy he abolished all inland customs dues. This infuriated the English merchants even more because they foresaw that their competitive advantage would be wiped out. They decided the nawab must go and so began a new conspiracy.

The nawab was, however, made of stern stuff and would not give way peacefully. He took up arms to defend the kingdom he had bought and worked an alliance with the nawab wazir (a combination governor and prime minister) of neighboring Oudh province, who was then entertaining the Mughal emperor, a refugee from Delhi. The allies met the English at Buxar late in 1764 and were defeated. The result was the Treaty of 1765, by which the Mughal emperor bestowed the diwany of Bengal, Bihar, and Orissa upon the company—the diwany was the civil administration of the province, especially its revenue administration.

This put the company in a different position. It held legal authority under a trading charter from the English Crown and political authority for an extensive tract within the Mughal Empire by virtue of a treaty and an appointment from the emperor. The Treaty of Buxar also involved the company in an offensive and defensive alliance with the nawab wazir of Oudh and in a joint surety for the protection of the emperor. As diwan of Bengal the company was required to contribute a portion of the revenues of Bengal to the maintenance of the emperor. These were far-reaching obligations for a mercantile company, whose officers were experienced in trade but not in government or in judicial processes.

For several years the company tried to avoid the implications of its role as diwan by keeping in office a naib-diwan, or deputy, who was an experienced Indian official. But this did not work, as the naib-diwan held office only at the whim of the English, who were generally too grasping to allow themselves to be regulated by him. The president of the council at Fort William tried to control his colleagues, but he faced an almost hopeless task, both because Clive had set the precedent for taking vast presents and because the officers of the company were normally appointed under the patronage of the powerful directors back home. Rules to control these officials might be passed, but no one could enforce them against the appointees, often the nephews or cousins, of the leading shareholders and powerful directors of the company. Between 1765 and 1793 the rich province of Bengal verged on ruin because of the excesses and plunder practiced by the company and its officers.

Meanwhile conquest had been shown to be profitable to the company's battalions, for the officers, who received graded shares of the loot after each campaign, and for the senior company officials. Regiments in the field received batta, or double per diem, and as soon as a battalion was put in the employ of a native prince, or a would-be prince, its entire cost fell upon the prince.

Despite these attractive provisions the cost of military operations turned out each year to be greater than the profits from the year's acquisitions for the company, though the officers of the company may have gained a great deal on their personal accounts. Like the Red Queen, the company discovered it had to run in order to stand still. There was, however, one important change. Prior to 1765 the company had sent specie from England each year in order to buy the goods desired. After 1765 it was never again necessary to export specie from England; Bengal revenues formed the "investment" and supplied much of the cost of wars in other parts of India. Bengal also provided the opium, received along with the land tax, which was shipped to China as the staple of the Canton trade. The land tax had to be increased to provide the maximum, despite a profound lack of information on the nature of the Indian revenue systems, the character of tenures, the concept of property in the Indian setting, and the value of the land as a commodity, if indeed in India it was a commodity.[55]

The company feared reliance upon native agency. The officers believed natives would lie, hide their records, understate the value of the land, and pay far less than the taxable capacity. In order to get rapidly at a fair market value upon which to base the revenue demand, they decided to employ the method of auction of zamindari rights on an annual basis. The assumption was that the natives, knowing the true worth of various estates and tracts, would bid as high as was feasible in order to win the right to collect the land revenue on behalf of the company, keeping for themselves a modest percentage as remuneration for the trouble of collection.

It soon became apparent, however, that annual auction was a noxious device. Speculators, rack renters, and others bid at the auctions in the hope of making a killing during the year they held the rights. The agrarian system was gravely upset, and the ryots, or cultivators, were subjected to unprecedented oppression. The company then experimented with a three-year auction, hoping that a longer interest in the estate would cause the zamindar to treat the cultivators with consideration. The results were negligible. British officials were then used to assess and collect the land revenue, but this, too, was a disaster, as the English officials were uninformed. A retreat was hastily beaten to the auction system, and in 1791 Lord Cornwallis, the new governor of Bengal, ordered that plans to settle the system of land revenue be made. Cornwallis was a Whig and favored an arrangement with a landed aristocracy. The outcome was the permanent Settlement of 1793, by which the company confirmed in fee simple, as owners of the land, the zamindars who held the land at that moment, as a result of the last auction. This wiped out any rights to the land, whatever they may have been, of all cultivators and

[55] Neale, "Land Is To Rule"; Embree, "Landholding in India and British Institutions"; Ranjit Guha, *A Rule of Property for Bengal* (Paris, 1963); Stokes, *English Utilitarians and India*.

intermediaries in Bengal, Bihar, and Orissa, making all cultivators tenants at will. It also confirmed that the new zamindar-landlords were to pay in perpetuity to the company the annual land revenue they had paid in the last fiscal year preceding the Settlement. Any gains in landed values or increases in rents were to accrue to the zamindars. A revolution in the landed rights of a vast area had been effected by decree.

Cornwallis also decreed that the entire superior decision-making organization was to be staffed solely by English officials, for he did not trust native agency. And he created a new, dual ladder of civil and criminal courts with English magistrates—company officers who might or might not have had any legal training—who were to be advised by native councilors, both Hindu and Muslim, on relevant points in indigenous law. The magistrate was not, however, bound by such advice. On this basis a hodgepodge of English law, local custom, snatches of Islamic law, and *dhyabhaga* Hindu law (one of two major systems of traditional, personal law), mixed with precedent from other courts, slowly grew up to become the bulk of what we know as Anglo-Indian law.[56] It did of course contain a fair admixture of basic English legal doctrines, such as the equality of all who appeared before the bench, a doctrine contrary to Hindu law, which had never dreamed that a Brahman and a Sudra could be judged by the same legal principles.

The company retained the Mughal system of provinces, districts, and circles, with English district officers and magistrates running the system in the supervisory and administrative positions. The clerical and subordinate officials continued to be Indian, holding essentially the same titles and generally the same duties as their predecessors had held for generations.[57] The major difference seems to have been that the district officers were increasingly regularized and systematized as interchangeable parts of a codified and rationalized administrative cadre, with handbooks designed to guide their behavior and duties and executive regulations handed down from above to control and bureaucratize them. Local authorities were simply not recognized by the British

---

[56] J. D. M. Derrett, "J. H. Nelson: A Forgotten Administrator-Historian of India," in Philips, *Historians of India, Pakistan and Ceylon*, 354–72.
[57] R. E. Frykenberg, *Guntur District* (Oxford, 1965).

administration or the British courts, and the latter steadily gathered all jurisdiction into their own hands. In every British territory the British held firmly to a monopoly of all force—military and police. These developments did not take place overnight but were major trends and processes set in motion by the Cornwallian reforms of 1793. There were, of course, some in the company who did not agree with these policies. These Orientalists argued that while the English must rule India, or parts of India, they should do so in accord with native ideas and institutions. The result was a struggle between the Anglicists and the Orientalists, which persisted from the days of Cornwallis down to the time of Macaulay, about 1835, when the Anglicists won out.[58]

A major landmark in this development was the revision in 1813 of the charter of the company, at which point the Anglicists and their allies, the missionaries, won a victory over the Orientalists.[59] After 1813 the trends were increasingly in favor of social change and reform along English lines. The Act of 1813 allowed active missionary enterprise for the first time in the company's territories and also enjoined the company to spend 100,000 rupees a year from its Indian revenues on education. There was disagreement for some years over the kind of education the Act desired to support, but in 1835 Macaulay laid down that high, Western education was what was wanted. His policy was accepted. By this time social reform by executive fiat had also been accepted as policy: for example, the practice of sati—the immolation of a widow on the funeral pyre of her husband—had been abolished.

Utilitarians were increasingly prominent in company circles, as were Evangelicals.[60] The triumph of the Industrial Revolution in England led to the destruction of the company's monopoly by 1833 and the opening of India to England's growing export trade. The merchant joined hands with the Evangelical and the Utili-

[58] Kopf, *British Orientalism and the Bengal Renaissance;* Robert I. Crane, "The Transfer of Western Education to India," in W. B. Hamilton, ed., *The Transfer of Institutions* (Durham, 1964), 108–38.

[59] B. T. McCully, *English Education and the Origins of Indian Nationalism* (New York, 1940).

[60] Stokes, *English Utilitarians and India;* Embree, *Charles Grant and British Rule in India;* Kopf, "Brahmo Samaj Intelligentsia and the Bengal Renaissance"; M. Mohar Ali, *The Bengali Reaction to Christian Missionary Activities* (Chittagong, 1965); Gauram Chattopadhyay, *Awakening in Bengal,* 1 (Calcutta, 1965); G. D. Bearce, *British Attitudes towards India* (London, 1961).

tarian, as well as with the avowed imperialist, to bring the "blessings" of European civilization—uplift, the gospel, and law and order—to benighted and backward peoples. The spread of British jurisdiction, Western education, and law were deemed natural adjuncts to the increased sale of the goods turned out by Manchester and Leeds. Civilizing and improving the native, prime goals of the Evangelicals and the Utilitarians, were also goals of the traveling salesman.

James Mill, a leading supporter of Bentham, was principal examiner at the India Office in London, where he wrote his influential *History of British India* and considerably influenced India policy. Moreover, Mountstuart Elphinstone, governor of Bombay, confessed a genuine intellectual debt to Bentham, as did other prominent Indian officials and settlement officers. Several of the important land-revenue settlement operations in India after 1813 carried a distinctively Benthamite economic philosophy. In fact, the so-called ryotwari settlement of most of southern India was rationalized in good part as being a Benthamite measure that struck down intermediaries between the state and the cultivator.[61]

It should be kept in mind that Utilitarianism contained a definite streak of "compulsion" in that its elitist assumption was that the Utilitarians knew what was good for society, whether the people involved did or not. This point of view fitted the British position in India nicely, since the executive branch that governed was in no way responsible to public opinion or popular control. The Orientalists were opposed to these arrogant, change-inducing philosophies, but their ideas were less and less prevalent. The well-known self-righteousness of the Victorian middle classes prepared the way for the emergence of racial determinism, while Social Darwinism provided a persuasive rationalization. The opinions of "heathen" and of "backward" peoples were no longer to stand in the way of progress.[62]

---

[61] Mukherjee, *Ryotwari System in Madras*. See also Devendra Panigrahi, *Charles Metcalfe in India* (Delhi, 1968), for a careful study of a prominent official who, while not a Utilitarian, was a liberal and a reformer during his tenure in India.

[62] For an aspect of the controversy over company policy in this setting, see N. G. Cassels, "The 'Compact' and the Pilgrim Tax: The Genesis of East India Company's

The push to enlighten Indians, to uplift them, and to reform their institutions added zeal to the commercial drive to open the country by means of steam navigation, railways, and roads, so that goods from Manchester and Leeds could circulate freely and civilize. To this end Lord Dalhousie announced his "doctrine of lapse," under which if a native ruler died without what the company considered a legitimate heir his state would lapse to the company's sovereign power. Dalhousie soon absorbed several principalities according to this dogma and mortally frightened many others. On each such occasion most of the native army and the administration of the deceased prince were disbanded, and retainers were left to shift for themselves. The old order reeled. At the same time new land-revenue settlements in annexed Oudh and in other portions of upper India wiped out many intermediaries between company and actual cultivator. Disgruntled nobles, zamindars, and petty chieftains multiplied. The reforming zeal of the British was at its height, at the expense of the older Indian privileged classes.

In 1856 the new Enfield rifle was issued, along with its greased cartridge, which had to be bitten before being placed in the weapon. Swiftly the story spread that the grease being used was either pig fat or cow fat. The one was completely defiling for Muslims, the other for Hindus. The sepoys were soon in a turmoil. Accumulated grievances among all those classes, groups, and sectors that felt threatened or dispossessed by the policies of the British or by changes that spread outward as accompaniments to British rule flared up around the spark provided to the native battalions by the greased cartridges. All who sought to return to the past, to prevent India from falling apart as the white man elbowed his way onto the scene, fell into an unstable coalition when the Bengal regiments mutinied in 1857.[63] Though the English were caught by complete surprise and suffered many uneasy

---

Social Policy," *Canadian Journal of History*, 7 (1972): 37–49; and Raghavan Iyer, "Utilitarianism and Empire in India," in T. R. Metcalf, ed., *Modern India* (London, 1971), 163–68.

[63] Sen, *Eighteen Fifty-Seven;* Chaudhuri, *Civil Rebellion in the Indian Mutiny;* Embree, *1857 in India;* R. C. Majumdar, *The Sepoy Mutiny and the Revolt of 1857* (Calcutta, 1957); John R. McLane, ed., *The Political Awakening in India* (Englewood Cliffs, 1970), 23–30.

moments, and despite the fact that for six months a number of districts in upper India were largely in the hands of mutineers or civil rebels, the Mutiny was easily put down. Madras was barely affected and the Bombay presidency only slightly more so. The recently annexed Punjab remained loyal and provided troops for the recapture of Delhi. No mercy was shown to any Indian believed to have been involved in any way. Caught in the middle were those Indians who had made an affirmative adjustment to British education and rule. They denounced the mutineers and supported British rule, but to the frightened and vengeful English community in India they were indistinguishable from the "niggers" who had slain their masters.

These Indians were the nascent educated Indian middle class, many of whom were graduates of colleges in and around Calcutta, where Hindu College, the first English-style college, had been opened in 1818. Calcutta, the largest city in India (ca. 250,000) and the seat of the company's government, had the widest range of European institutions.[64] There the Orientalist point of view had developed under Lord Wellesley. There Orientalists had founded the Asiatic Society of Bengal and sponsored research in the languages, culture, and history of the region. They had also supported the School Book Society and the School Society for the education of Indians. Many of them had been on the staff of the College at Fort William, which Lord Wellesley created for the training of the covenanted servants—the officers—of the company. From this nexus emerged the initial generation of Indian scholars trained in the English language, Western concepts, and modern techniques of academic investigation. Several among them founded Hindu College and lesser institutions to impart the new knowledge to their countrymen. From these activities emerged the new, Western-educated class and the rebirth of learning about India's past, a major development in the study of Indian languages and literatures and critical studies in Indology.

Among this knot of the new intelligentsia of Bengal were men like Ram Mohan Roy, the paradigm for the modernizing and re-

[64] See A. F. Salahuddin Ahmed, *Social Ideas and Social Change in Bengal* (Leiden, 1965), an important study of the English impact and of the varieties of Indian response.

forming interaction between Indians and Englishmen. Ram Mohan formed the Brahmo Samaj, a society proposing to reform Hinduism and strip it of its weaknesses and to rationalize its spirit and laws in conformity with the highest ideals of the European Enlightenment. The Brahmo Samaj came to be an important sect among the intelligentsia, but only for a distinct minority. Ram Mohan also demanded equality for Hindu women, a free press, representative institutions, and similar reforms. His views tended to be typical of the Bengali intellectuals up through the days of the Mutiny.[65]

India under the Crown

Debate over the character of the Mutiny began almost as soon as word reached London of the uprising at Meerut. Each faction and party sought to blame the other—though all could agree that the savage and barbaric natives were the worst fiends—for having caused the populace to revolt. By the time the Mutiny had been suppressed dozens of theories, allegations, and stereotypes had been advanced to explain what had happened and to guide imperial policy in the post-Mutiny period. That the natives were unreliable and must be kept in place was widely agreed upon; that the British in India must remain vigilant and keep their distance from the ever-dangerous natives became an unspoken assumption. For more than half a century the gulf between the imperial, ruling race and the subject peoples that had yawned so widely in 1857–58 was not bridged. As a direct consequence, moreover, the British began more systematically than ever to seek Indian supporters and clients who could be won over or attached by self-interest to imperial rule. This involved a delicate social calculus in which the rulers had constantly to weigh and assess kaleidoscopic shifts in class, communal, regional, and caste forces and relations as well as cost-benefit ratios. Errors in judgment and honest disagreements over

---

[65] See Kopf, "Brahmo Samaj Intelligentsia and the Bengal Renaissance"; N. S. Bose, *The Indian Awakening and Bengal* (Calcutta, 1960); S. D. Collet, *The Life and Letters of Raja Rammohan Roy* (London, 1900); B. B. Majumdar, *History of Political Thought: Rammohun to Dayananda* (Calcutta, 1934); and Iqbal Singh, *Rammohun Roy* (Bombay, 1958).

strategy or tactics were not uncommon. Each proconsul had his pet theories or favorite mix of clients to placate as well as enemies to keep off balance. Some were flexible and pragmatic; others came out to India with preconceived notions, racist assumptions, and old wives' tales embedded firmly in their heads. The great majority agreed that the natives had to be managed and manipulated—partly so as to keep them from again uniting against their overlords—but each official might well have tenacious ideas about how best to do the job. Meanwhile various sects, communities, castes, and other groups in India jostled each other for opportunities and competitive advantage. The modernization process was slowly changing India and in so doing was altering the opportunity structure, the professions, the nature of relevant knowledge, and the sanctions.

A prominent consequence of the Mutiny was the abolition of the company, which served as a scapegoat. Direct Crown rule through a secretary of state for India, who was a member of the British cabinet and responsible with it to Parliament, replaced the defunct company. The secretary of state headed a substantial bureaucracy at the India Office in Whitehall and was staffed by permanent civil servants. Subordinate to his instructions was a governor-general in council in Calcutta, normally serving a five-year term. His council consisted of nominated senior civil servants who were heads of the great departments of the government of India.[66] By the Act of 1858 this executive council was to be enlarged, for purposes of legislation, by the addition of six to twelve nominated members, half of whom were to be nominated nonofficials. The governor-general had the veto power over all acts of the legislative council, and the secretary of state for India had the power to veto any legislation of the government of India or of the local governments, or provinces, of which he disapproved. It was also made clear that the governor-general in council was obligated to give effect to any legislation required by the secretary of state.

The governor-general was aided by an imposing bureaucracy in the secretariat in Calcutta, also organized on a departmental

[66] B. B. Misra, *The Administrative History of India, 1834–1947* (New York, 1970).

basis. The executive council was not a cabinet, for the governor-general conducted the business of each department with the member in charge of that department and with its secretary and permanent undersecretaries. Secretaries and members did "minute" on the files on all department issues, and the ponderous circulation of these linked files for "minuting" was at the heart of the governing procedures. Members served in council for a few years as the capstone of a successful career in the Indian Civil Service (ICS). The secretaries and undersecretaries normally held much longer tenure in their permanent posts and gave the various departments a continuity that could be stultifying. This was equally true of the India Office in Whitehall, for the secretary of state was a party appointee, normally in office for a few years only and knowing very little about India.

Each province, if it ranked as a presidency, was directed by a governor and a council; if not a presidency, the province was headed by a lieutenant governor. Governors were political or patronage appointees from London and had the right to correspond directly with the secretary of state. The lieutenant governors, by contrast, were appointed by the governor-general, with the approval of the secretary of state, from among the members of the ICS. They could not correspond directly with the secretary of state, did not have a council, and were more directly supervised by Calcutta. Each district in British India was under a district officer and a district magistrate, both from the ICS. Groups of four or five districts were under a deputy commissioner. Each province had a high court and one or two circuit courts.[67]

The post-Mutiny era witnessed an intensification of the systematizing and unifying tendencies of the government. Calcutta increasingly brought the district administration and the local governments under its supervision. People in all parts of the land found themselves subject to uniform codes of law and civil procedure. Macaulay had started the codification of the laws in the

[67] On the civil service in India and administrative centralization, see Misra, *Administrative History of India;* Bradford Spangenberg "Recruitment to the Indian Civil Service," *Journal of Asian Studies,* 30 (1971): 341–60; Singh, *Problems and Policies of the British in India;* and N. C. Roy, *The Civil Service in India* (Calcutta, 1960).

1830s, but this trend came to its peak in the 1860s and 1870s.

Administrative unification and uniform judicial codification were accompanied by the steady growth toward the physical unification of the subcontinent. Railways, highways, postal systems, and the telegraph unified India in unprecedented degree. By 1900 India had more railway mileage than any other nation in Asia. Concomitantly the monetization of the economy went on rapidly, and a true national market was created, with many aspects of the economic infrastructure being constructed—banks, insurance companies, a national system of credit for major commercial undertakings, a stock exchange, warehousing facilities, and steam navigation. This process was, however, uneven and at times haphazard, in part because the doctrine of government was laissez faire and noninterference carried at times to an extreme.[68] The sectors of the economy most readily linked to export and the world market were the most rapidly and highly developed, while those sectors of little or no interest to the export trade tended to be bypassed or left behind. The Empire was primarily concerned with trade and the raw materials for the metropolitan economy of Britain. The colonies experienced development in production of raw materials and cash crops that entered into the export trade. Cash crops were also important because their sale facilitated payment of rent to landlord or revenue to government. This monetized the agrarian economy.

Post-Mutiny policy, however, was not intended to change India or to push social reform. There was a distinct tendency to support the so-called aristocracy and the landlords because they were seen as a prop to British rule. The queen's proclamation, at the end of the Mutiny, promised that Indians would be able to practice their religions without interference, and their property and other traditional rights were guaranteed. Native princes were now assured that they could adopt heirs to whom their thrones

---

[68] There were of course paradoxes and anomalies in the application of laissez faire doctrine in any colony. The mother country had economic interests in the colony that demanded to be served and upon occasion overturned the "rules" of laissez faire, leading to paradoxical situations. India's late-nineteenth-century history is studded with such instances. Singh, *Problems and Policies of the British in India,* cites a number, as does Blair Kling in *Blue Mutiny* (Philadelphia, 1966). There is a growing literature exposing the contradictions in imperial policy toward India in this respect. The Indian nationalists were, of course, infuriated by such inconsistency.

could descend. Greater reliance upon indirect rule and the status quo became the order of the day. It was remarked that the Indian communities had not cooperated effectively in the Mutiny, and perspicacious officials opined that natural divisions among the Indians might be perpetuated, for a united India would endanger British supremacy.

The British nonetheless continued to modernize India and, as has been noted, to unify the country. As a result Indians could increasingly rub shoulders, travel about, and exchange ideas, facilitating that social mobilization which Karl Deutsch regards as crucial to nation building.[69] In all parts of British India the people faced increasingly standardized institutions, schools, public agencies, and other facilities. English was everywhere the language of administration and the colleges. The high schools had to instruct in English because the matriculation exam required for admission to college was administered in English. Only a small percentage of Indians graduated from high school in the nineteenth century, and a smaller percentage—under five per cent—went on to college, but this was a critically important minority and was spread widely in cities and towns in all parts of the subcontinent. English was the lingua franca of this new educated and professional class, and ideas circulated widely. All who took the B.A. or B.Law degrees had been exposed to the same basic set of ideas—the standard curriculum of mid-Victorian England, with its literary bias and its emphasis upon the preparation of the English governing classes for their responsibilities.[70]

After 1861, partly because of pressure from Indian nationalists, steps were taken to enlarge the central legislature and to create or enlarge the provincial, or local, legislative councils. In 1881 Lord Ripon requested, through his Local Self-Government Act, the creation of municipal and district boards with elected majorities. He felt that Indians must be trained in parliamentary institutions and ought to secure that training at local levels. After 1882 regular participation in electoral processes, though on a limited property and literacy franchise, spread steadily more widely among Indians.

[69] Karl Deutsch, "Social Mobilization and Political Development," *American Political Science Review*, 55 (1961): 493–514.

[70] See Ellen McDonald, "English Education and Social Reform in Late Nineteenth Century Bombay," *Journal of Asian Studies*, 35 (1966): 453–70.

The Western-educated class looked upon such institutions as the natural corollary of British rule and demanded that all legislative bodies be rapidly Indianized on an elective basis. They also demanded broader powers for such legislatures. Even the liberal English, however, favored a very cautious policy in Indianization or in broadening the franchise or the powers of the legislatures.

The Indian Councils Act of 1891 enlarged the governor-general's legislative council and gave it a membership partly chosen on the basis of an indirect and very restricted franchise. Legislative councils, again with highly restricted franchise, were also created for the major provinces. Soon thereafter the lieutenant governors were given councils. All of these bodies continued to have majorities of nominated members. Many Englishmen, especially officials, were unconvinced that the educated classes had the right to claim to speak for any broad constituency or to exercise any wider powers. From their point of view the real issue was how much authority could safely be transferred to Indians without endangering British rule.

The British were seeking clients, reliable supporters, and a means by which their government could secure the opinions of the various interests in Indian society; the Indian nationalists were seeking meaningful installments in the transfer of power. In this context an amusing and unedifying quarrel broke out over the relative representative character of the new Western-educated Indian middle classes, whose pretensions were sneered at by most of the British, while officers in the ICS alleged in a pontifical fashion that they more nearly represented the best interests of India's "voiceless millions" than did the educated Indian classes. In this polemic war senior ICS officers such as H. H. Risley analyzed the Indian body politic intensively and came to the conclusion that it was virtually impossible to create constituencies for which equitable and natural representation could be secured in the normal course of events. Too many diverse interests—communal, caste, sect, and economic—were said to exist in each logical constituency to make it possible to devise a franchise that would produce a fair or equitable representation. This academic splintering of the body politic infuriated the nationalists, who retorted that it was clearly a mere tactic of *divide et impera*.

Modernization, Nationalism, and Development

All these changes helped lay the basis for nationhood and nationalism in South Asia and were also part of the ongoing process of development and modernization,[71] even though haphazard, uneven, and often unintentional. India was slowly being modernized, and by 1900 the crucial issues were who was to benefit from the process and who would guide the course of development. The Indian educated middle classes were increasingly determined that they should gain access to the levers of power and have greater participation in the process of modernization.

The British, of course, had a different view of this matter. They looked upon the Indian educated classes as clerks and office menials in their subordinate services. Indian expectations and ambitions had grown rapidly, though not necessarily in a monolithic or unified fashion. There were sectoral, regional, communal, and other divergencies and contrary trends among the new-style elites and emerging nationalist leaders. These were in part reflections of ideological disagreements, in part differences over strategy and tactics, and in part rivalries over the "loaves and fishes" of office. They also reflected differential types of response to European impact and European ideas.[72] In general, however, educated Indians wanted an ever larger voice in decision-making, and given

[71] The term "modernization," as used here, is intended to be value free. I do not argue that modernization makes people or institutions "better" or "worse," that modernization is a process that was created in any corner of the globe. Hence I do not give modernization a cultural bias. Japan today may well be more modern than Spain or Belgium. Nor is race considered relevant. I do not imply that people, or societies, are better or happier if modern. There are different ways of organizing life and of aggregating interests and values, but one way is not held to be better than the other—that is a purely subjective value judgment. The modernizing process characteristically leads to uses of time, energy, skills, and resources different from the uses typical in traditional polities. These are simply different ways of sorting people, and they have different consequences, which can, with a bit of care, be specified.

[72] See Robert I. Crane, "Leadership of the Congress Party," in R. L. Park and Irene Tinker, eds., *Leadership and Political Institutions in India* (Princeton, 1959), 169–87; Robert I. Crane, "Divergent Developments in Indian Nationalism, 1895–1905," in R. Sakai, ed., *Studies on Asia, 1962* (Lincoln, 1962), 1–15; and J. H. Broomfield, "The Regional Elites: A Theory of Modern Indian History," *Indian Economic and Social History Review*, 3 (1966): 279–91. Anie Seal, *The Emergence of Indian Nationalism* (Cambridge, 1968), is primarily concerned with the uneven development of, and competition among, various Indian elites.

the presuppositions of a British-style administration and education these expectations focused on the composition and powers of the legislatures and on Indianization of the superior public services, especially the all-powerful ICS. So Indian nationalists were brought face to face with the crucial British monopoly of power. In the ensuing controversy each side excoriated the other, heaped obloquy upon the claims and status of the other side, and cast about feverishly for allies, supporters, and clients. From 1885 to 1935 the political history of India was the history of an exceedingly intricate interaction between elites and counterelites as well as other power or status-seeking groups of Indians and their British rulers. This competition played into the hands of the senior administrators, who controlled the imperial levers of power and sought, with greater or lesser skill, to detach elements of the opposition from the nationalist camp and render them neutral or pro-British. Concessions, repression, constitutional awards, communal electorates and reserved seats, differential access to government jobs and scholarships, and manipulation of the qualifications for the franchise were all used at one time or another in managing, diverting, wooing, or rewarding groups, classes, and categories of potential supporters of British rule.[73] Not all civil servants were equally interested or involved in such manipulation, while some officials were opposed to it on grounds of principle or strategy, fearing that any move might backfire against the British or that the allies won by these means might prove to be too costly and embarrassing. The situation was further complicated by controversy between London and Calcutta, or later between London and New Delhi—where the imperial seat of government was located in 1911—as decision-makers in the two centers often had different angles of vision and responded to different sets of pressures or interests. Normally muted, on occasion the disagreement between Britain and India over policy or tactics broke out into more or less overt

[73] An excellent analysis of such manipulation is in Broomfield, *Elite Conflict in a Plural Society*. See also, Dietmar Rothermund, "Emancipation or Re-Integration: The Politics of G. K. Gokhale and H. H. Risely," in D. A. Low, ed., *Soundings in Modern South Asian History* (Berkeley, 1968), 131–58; D. A. Low, "The Government of India and the First Non-Cooperation Movement—1920–1922," *Journal of Asian Studies*, 25 (1966): 241–59; Peter Reeves, "Landlords and Party Politics in the United Provinces," in Low, *Soundings in Modern South Asian History*, 261–93; and Barrier, *Punjab Alienation of Land Bill*.

controversy.[74] In general the decision-makers in India argued that London must trust their judgment and support their decisions, though the secretary of state and his advisers often reminded the Indian official that Whitehall was legally and morally supreme.

The nationalists, especially the Congress party, found it necessary to secure as broad a base and as much popular following as possible. The government of India would surely pay no attention to their claims or petitions unless they could demonstrate their representative character. After 1890 and increasingly after 1905 this led to experiments with popular politics, mass contacts, and the politicization of broad sectors of the population. Bal G. Tilak was one of the first nationalist leaders to make serious efforts to secure a mass following and to apply pressure to the British raj to grant concessions. Tilak led the younger, more militant Hindu nationalists, who demanded self-rule and flirted with extremist measures. Unfortunately for the future of nationalist politics, Tilak and some of his colleagues found it easy and expedient to reach a mass audience by using the familiar symbols and myths of Hinduism. This kind of appeal worked fairly well with Hindu listeners, but it sowed the seeds of Muslim alienation and growing political separatism. The politics of "scarcity," which led to quarrels over the allocation of resources, exacerbated the fissures and hostilities that had been fanned by an appeal to religious symbols in the search for popular support.

The appeal of the extremists and Hindu militants was, however, fairly limited. Certain sectors of society responded, others did not. By the beginning of the First World War it was apparent that more than extremism, militant Hindu sentiment and a dash of terrorism would be needed to secure real concessions or substantial progress toward nationalist goals.[75] During the First World War M. K.

[74] Stephen Koss, *John Morley at the India Office* (New Haven, 1969). See also Barrier, "The Arya Samaj and Congress Politics in the Punjab," for a discussion of the controversy between Morley and Minto and between Minto and the lieutenant governor of the Punjab over strategy and tactics in dealing with various wings of the nationalist movement.

[75] On extremists and terrorists, see M. A. Buch, *Rise and Growth of Indian Militant Nationalism* (Baroda, 1940); Haridas and Uma Mukherjee, *Sri Aurobindo's Political Thought* (Calcutta, 1958); O. P. Goyal, *Modern Indian Political Thought* (Allahabad, 1964); and Haridas and Uma Mukherjee, *Bipin Chandra Pal and India's Struggle for Swaraj* (Calcutta, 1958).

Gandhi returned to India from South Africa, where he had gained valuable experience and tested his political doctrines. By 1919 he had moved to the forefront of Indian nationalism. In 1920 Gandhi captured control of the Indian National Congress and rewrote its constitution to make it a mass-based party.

The Gandhian Era

Gandhi ushered in mass politics, the politics of self-help, and politics based upon social-welfare ideals for the transformation of the conditions of life of the poverty-stricken masses. His religion was to express itself in "uplift" and in political struggle for the amelioration of the lives of the Indian people. His sincerity, humility, and simplicity caught the popular imagination, and he was apotheosized as the Mahatma, winning for the Congress a mass following it had never had before. His reorganization of the Congress included creation of several self-help and village-improvement societies and organizations, such as the All India Village Spinners Society. In all of this Gandhi stressed national unity around the goals of Swadeshi and Swaraj—homemade goods and self-rule or independence.[76]

Gandhi strove earnestly for Hindu-Muslim amity, but that goal eluded his best efforts, in part because too many factors in the Indian scene were arrayed against him and in part because Muslim politicians had learned how to exploit Muslim religious fears and hopes in order to win a mass following, just as the Hindu militants had done in the 1890s.[77] Communal politics had, since the Morley-Minto reforms of 1909, revolved around reservation of seats, weightage, communal representation, and similar privileges. When necessary, unscrupulous politicians went to the masses to

---

[76] There is a vast proliferation of materials on Gandhi. A sample of some of the better titles would include M. K. Gandhi, *An Autobiography* (New York, 1957); M. K. Gandhi, *Satyagraha in South Africa* (Ahmedabad, 1950); H. A. Jack, ed., *The Gandhi Reader* (Bloomington, 1956); B. R. Nanda, *Mahatma Gandhi*, (Boston, 1959); Indira Rothermund, *The Philosophy of Restraint* (Bombay, 1963); P. F. Power, ed., *The Meanings of Gandhi* (Honolulu, 1971); and Joan Bondurant, *Conquest of Violence, The Gandhian Philosophy* (Princeton, 1958).

[77] Khalid bin Sayeed, *Pakistan, The Formative Phase* (Karachi, 1960); W. C. Smith, "The 'Ulama' in Indian Politics," in Metcalf, *Modern India*, 103–12.

rouse street mobs to riot in support of their demands. This was, of course, a game any clique or faction could play, for all sorts of ends. Unfortunately it could equally well get out of hand, leading to truly explosive riots, looting, and an intensification of communal hostility.

Against this melancholy trend the National Congress set itself to promote a policy of secularism and material improvement of the conditions of the people in the context of distributive justice and equal opportunity. As the efforts to acquire a mass following broadened the base of the Congress, its policies and tactics became increasingly popularized. This led to the emergence of alliances with class-oriented groups and organizations, such as the developing peasant unions and trade unions and a mass-contacts program that was in part inspired by the new left-wing and Fabian-socialist faction within the ranks of the Congress. By 1931 these tendencies had led to serious intraparty quarrels that Gandhi's leadership alone had been able to contain. The agrarian crisis, brought on by the deepening world depression, only intensified the strains and the controversies over Congress policy vis-à-vis landless laborers, agrarian reform, trade unions, and mass membership. The Gandhian "reformist" wing had a clear majority in the Congress, but this did not avert conflict over strategy and tactics with the socialists, who were in despair over their inability to prevail in the face of Gandhian doctrine or the size of his following. The Gandhians insisted upon a broad front united around nonviolent civil resistance, with membership in the Congress as a crucial prerequisite and all other affiliations being subordinated. The young socialists favored independent class organizations, each with its own program, linked in an alliance with the Congress around defined goals. The Congress sought to dampen ideological differences under a common struggle for Swaraj and the general welfare, while the socialists sought to sharpen class and ideological understanding and to enroll peasants in politically conscious peasant organizations against the British and the landlords.[78]

---

[78] See, for example, Peter Reeves, "The Politics of Order," *Journal of Asian Studies*, 25 (1966): 261–74; John Haithcox, "Left Wing Unity and the Indian Nationalist Movement," *Modern Asian Studies*, 3 (1969): 17–56; "Kisan Sabhas in Bihar and Gujarat," in McLane, *Political Awakening in India*, 157–60; T. A. Rusch,

Meanwhile the Government of India Act of 1935 came into effect as a consequence of protracted struggles and negotiations, and the Congress finally decided to contest the elections, as did the Muslim League, which was now being rejuvenated by Muhammed Ali Jinnah. The Congress won a resounding victory at the polls, while the Muslim League did not capture very many of the seats reserved for Muslims. For complex reasons the Congress refused to form coalition ministries with the League except under conditions that the League found galling, and the last opportunity for cooperation between the Congress and the Muslim League had passed away. The Congress governed in eight of British India's eleven provinces, but the League was increasingly sullen and bitter. Communal riots and related incidents grew in number and significance.

In 1939 the war broke out in Europe, and the viceroy proclaimed India at war. The Congress protested bitterly that responsible Indian leaders had not been consulted, and as a result the Congress ministries resigned in all eight provinces, which passed under the emergency rule of their governors. Soon thereafter several governors called upon the Muslim League members of the provincial legislatures to form interim ministries, which stayed in office until the beginning of 1946. The Congress was in oblivion, and the League was in office. Many Indian writers have since stigmatized as folly the Congress decision to resign in 1939.

In 1942 the Congress passed the Quit India Declaration, and the entire high command was promptly locked up in jail the next morning for the duration of hostilities. This action had been the culmination of long and tortured debates over the Cripps Mission, which had offered the Indians an allegedly significant advance toward self-government after the war in return for participation in the war effort. The Cripps offer was, however, hedged by several crippling limitations and transferred virtually nothing to Indians until after the war. Certain clauses of the offer could be read to imply the partition of India into several successor states, and

---

"Dynamics of Socialist Leadership in India," in Park and Tinker, *Leadership and Political Institutions in India*, 188–210.

Indian nationalist leaders were not prepared to sign any agreement that could result in the vivisection of India.

By the time the war ended the situation had changed. Britain was no longer a major imperial power, and a Labour government had come to office on a record of repeated promises to free India. Very quickly thereafter real measures were taken for the actual transfer of power. Though the negotiations were vexed, painful, and confused, with everyone talking at once and in contradictory terms, the new viceroy, Lord Mountbatten, kept to a firm timetable and shoved his hesitant colleagues sometimes unwittingly ahead along the road to independence. Time was rapidly running out for British power to solve the many dilemmas it now faced. Mountbatten realized this, and he gave the actors three months in which to clear away the debris of two centuries. Amazingly, by the date set—August 15, 1947—everything that had to be done had been done, India was partitioned, and two new, sovereign nations came into being.[79]

[79] There is a vast and growing literature on the transfer of power. Much of it is tendentious, some is almost pure fiction. Among the better titles are V. P. Menon, *The Transfer of Power in India* (Princeton, 1957); Alan Campbell-Johnson, *Mission with Mountbatten* (New York, 1953); Lord Louis Mountbatten, *Time Only to Look Forward* (London, 1949); Penderel Moon, *Divide and Quit* (Berkeley, 1962); and Michael Brecher, *The Struggle for Kashmir* (New York, 1953). Michael Brecher, *Nehru, A Political Biography* (London, 1959), has several chapters on events leading up to and surrounding independence. There is also a growing literature of biographies and autobiographies of men in England and India who played a prominent role in the final years of British rule and the transfer of power to Indian or Pakistani hands. See N. C. Chaudhuri, *Autobiography of an Unknown Indian* (New York, 1951); E. M. Forster, *Hill of Devi* (Harmondsworth, 1965); Martin Gilbert, *Servant of India, A Study of Imperial Rule* (London, 1966); V. C. Joshi, ed., *Lajpat Rai, Autobiographical Writings*, 1 (Delhi, 1965); E. S. Montagu, *An Indian Diary* (London, 1930); Jawaharlal Nehru, *Toward Freedom, An Autobiography* (Boston, 1963); Stanley Reed, *The India I Knew, 1897-1947* (London, 1952); J. A. Simon, *Retrospect: The Memoirs of Viscount Simon* (London, 1952); Frederick Sykes, *From Many Angles, An Autobiography* (London, 1942); Edward Wakefield, *Past Imperative, My Life in India, 1927-1947* (London, 1966); P. K. Rao, *The Right Hon. V. S. Srinivasa Sastri, A Political Biography* (Bombay, 1963); B. R. Nanda, *The Nehrus, Motilal and Jawaharlal* (London, 1962); Frederick W. Smith, Earl of Birkenhead, *Halifax: The Life of Lord Halifax* (London, 1965); Maulana Abul Kalam Azad, *India Wins Freedom* (New York, 1960); S. C. Bose, *The Indian Struggle, 1935-42* (Calcutta, 1952); Hector Bolitho, *Jinnah, Creator of Pakistan* (New York, 1954); Sunder Shyam, *Political Life of Pandit Govind Ballabh Pant* (Lucknow, 1960); N. D. Parikh, *Sardar Vallabhbhai Patel* (Ahmedabad, 1953-56); Rajendra Prasad, *Autobiography* (Bombay, 1957); A. C. Banerjee, ed., *Indian Constitutional Documents* (Calcutta, 1945-49); B. L. Grover, ed., *A Documentary Study of British Policy toward Indian Nationalism, 1885-1909* (Delhi, 1967); and Philips, *Evolution of India and Pakistan*.

Independence, Partition, and Development

Independence for the two new nations brought a spate of problems along with high hopes and some tragedy.[80] The rhetoric of the preindependence struggle had adumbrated a series of nation-building, welfare-oriented goals and promises for the future. It had been assumed that the departure of the British would solve many problems and usher in an era of rapid economic growth, equal opportunity, distributive justice, and social harmony. Twenty-five years later it is possible to recognize the grave complexities and structural difficulties that had to be faced and overcome before the premises of the struggle for freedom could hope to be fulfilled. Even if a number of the hurdles that have stood in the way were colonial legacies, they were not so easily eliminated as was assumed in 1947. Moreover there was the largely unforeseen problem that the colonial system had tended to replicate itself or at least to leave parts of its structure and value system behind after the British departed. A large bureaucracy and many party politicians, as well as others in elite circles, had internalized values and attitudes of the British. Many politicians had learned only too well the kinds of politics that had served in British hands to minimize change and maintain a safe status quo. The gap between the governors and the governed was in some ways as great after 1947 as it had been before.[81]

Unlike Pakistan, India had a relatively vigorous parliamentary tradition, a strong, broadly based national political party, a lively and rapidly growing middle class, and several major urban and commercial centers. Politicization and social mobilization had been carried much further in India than in Pakistan and proceeded at a more rapid pace after 1947. But at the time of independence some eighty-four per cent of the Indian population were rural, and fourteen per cent were reported to be literate. The annual income per person was said to be approximately $53.00 in

---

[80] There are interesting books on the tragic events surrounding Partition in 1947. Khushwant Singh has a very perceptive novel, *Train to Pakistan* (New York, 1956). Moon, *Divide and Quit*, is a biographical account. See also H. G. Alexander, *New Citizens of India* (London, 1951).

[81] Fanon, *Wretched of the Earth,* has a very perceptive discussion of postcolonial regimes in this respect.

terms of real U.S. dollar equivalents. In 1947 there was not a single establishment that could manufacture even a one-horsepower engine. Yields per acre, for most crops, were among the lowest in the world. The average farmer worked a holding often fragmented into two to four plots, of approximately 4.5 acres each, and was in debt and frequently failed to get out of debt at any time in his adult life. The village—there were about 550,000 in India—had no electricity, no safe drinking water, no sanitation system, and usually no school. The economy of India was relatively undiversified, with more than fifty per cent of the gross national product coming from agriculture. Much of the so-called industrial sector in 1947 consisted of rural industry for processing agricultural raw materials, such as sugar mills or jute mills. And India's steel mills could not produce more than two million tons of steel a year. India also produced cigarettes, soap, matches, cotton textiles, hides, and a few other items of an industrial character. Cash crops, however, were the staple of India's export economy. Due to the exigencies of the Partition, which was along religious lines, almost all of the existing factories and processing facilities happened to fall within the Republic of India and very few within Pakistan. Thus the latter, in 1947, was even more rural and much less industrialized than India.

As there was no machine-tool industry in India, a major problem was the achievement of sustained growth in industry and a self-generating capacity. In the early years of independence it was necessary to import a large proportion of almost any item that was fabricated, and so foreign currency earnings were eaten up. Because agricultural production was low and increasing slowly, while the rate of population increase was high (2.4 per cent per annum), India also had to import food grains, particularly in those years in which the monsoon rains failed. This further depleted scarce foreign exchange.

Capital for investment in new productive capacity or in improved farming procedures was in short supply and not being aggregated in adequate amounts. Fiscal policy failed to guarantee rapid mobilization of resources for high-level investment. Agricultural incomes were not subject to income tax because the tradition inherited from the British had been to tax the land but not the income from the land. In effect many affluent sectors were able virtually to avoid substantial contribution to the costs of national economic development.

There were a series of schemes for limiting the size of landholdings—allegedly to facilitate redistribution to the landless—but such plans were greatly delayed by tests in the courts or vitiated by loopholes in the phrasing. Tenants and share croppers continued, by and large, to operate under constraints that robbed them of all incentive to work hard, economize, or grow more. In the years since independence it would appear that the bottom forty per cent of the agrarian order have experienced almost no improvement in their conditions of life. Even the middle thirty per cent have undergone less amelioration of living conditions than had been widely expected in 1947. These facts have contributed to what Myron Weiner has called "the politics of scarcity."[82]

Shortly after independence the Indian government created a constituent assembly. By the beginning of 1950 the assembly had prepared a lengthy constitution, modeled partly after the U.S. Constitution and in good part indebted to the British parliamentary system. Under this Constitution India is a federal republic with universal adult suffrage. Certain powers are given to the union, or center, others belong to the several states, while still others are on the concurrent list. Some kinds of revenue go to the union, some to the states, and some are shared. There is a supreme court, and high courts are set up in the states. The president has special powers (borrowed from the Government of India Act of 1935) to intervene and administer any state if he certifiies that the normal state administration has broken down. The government of India is parliamentary in form, with a prime minister, cabinet,

[82] Myron Weiner, *The Politics of Scarcity* (Chicago, 1962), *passim*. On economic development problems and prospects, see S. K. Bose, *Some Aspects of Indian Economic Development*, 1 (Delhi, 1962); R. J. Braibanti and J. J. Spengler, eds., *Administration of Economic Development in India* (Durham, 1963); John P. Lewis, *Quiet Crisis in India* (Washington, 1962); Wilfred Malenbaum, *Prospects for Indian Development* (New York, 1962); A. B. Das, *The Indian Economy, Its Growth and Problems* (8th ed.; Calcutta, 1963); Kusum Nair, *Blossoms in the Dust* (New York, 1963); S. K. Basu, ed., *Studies in Economic Problems* (New York, 1965); K. N. Raj, *Indian Economic Growth, Performances and Perspectives* (New Delhi, 1965); P. T. Bauer, *Indian Economic Policy and Development* (Bombay, 1965); and George Rosen, *Democracy and Economic Change in India* (Berkeley, 1967).

and an upper and lower house very similar in powers to the British Parliament.[83]

In India, however, there has so far been what political scientists call a one-party-dominant system, in which although parliamentary government, secret ballot, and all of the significant institutions of democracy—with distinctly Indian garb—have been assiduously adhered to, one political party has dominated the union government and a majority of the state governments since independence. That party has of course been the party of Gandhi and Nehru, the Congress party. Compared to the Congress party the opposition parties have been small and fragmented. The Congress party has acted as an umbrella party, occupying the center of the political spectrum and leaving the right and left fringes to several small factions and parties, some of which have been regional rather than all-India in scope. Being the party in power, the Congress has also been in the best position to influence elections by use of patronage, manipulation of careerist ambitions of regional political leaders, and utilization of the bandwagon effect. The Congress has been in the best all-India position to aggregate interests and to act to meet them.

Given the constraints of a scarcity economy and a rate of population growth that threatened to consume a good deal of the increase in the gross national product (4 per cent per annum at best), the satisfaction of consumer expectations and the balancing of such demands to maintain a successful electoral coalition have required supreme political skill, finesse, and timing. Nor has it been possible at all times for the Congress to succeed in so delicate a set of balancing operations. The party's continued electoral victories,

[83] On the Indian political system, see N. D. Palmer, *The Indian Political System* (Boston, 1961); C. H. Philips, ed., *Politics and Society in India* (New York, 1962); Walter Hauser, "Society and Politics in Modern India," in Robert I. Crane, ed., *Southern Asia* (Durham, 1968), 28–47; J. D. M. Derrett, *Religion, Law and the State in India* (New York, 1968); S. A. Kochanek, *The Congress Party of India* (Princeton, 1968); R. Bhaskaran, *Sociology of Politics, Tradition and Politics in India* (New York, 1967); W. H. Morris-Jones, *The Government and Politics of India* (2d ed.; London, 1967); R. L. Park, *India's Political System* (Englewood Cliffs, 1967); B. R. Nayar, *Minority Politics in the Punjab* (Princeton, 1966); Ram Gopal, *Indian Muslims, A Political History* (Bombay, 1964); Myron Weiner, *India's Two Political Cultures* (Cambridge, Mass., 1964); Paul Brass, *Factional Politics in an Indian State* (Berkeley, 1965); and R. L. Hardgrave, *The Dravidian Movement* (Bombay, 1965).

however, are testimony to its abilities along these lines as compared with the competition.

The Congress has fortunately had charismatic leadership to help it over many a difficult hour; it has had access to more and better propaganda mechanisms than have many of its rivals; and there has often been or appeared to be an external threat to unite India's millions behind the party that won freedom. For years there has been the presence of hostile Pakistan, led by generals and armed by the United States through SEATO and CENTO. And after 1962 there was the very palpable danger from Tibet of an all-too-convincing Chinese Red Army. After the 1971 Bangladesh war had apparently allayed the overt threat from Pakistan, relations with the United States deteriorated as a result of that country's bias in favor of Pakistan. Subsequently the government of India claimed to have evidence of substantial activity in India by the U.S. Central Intelligence Agency, all of it said to be detrimental to India's security and national well-being. This threat, openly denounced by the government of India, soon assumed large proportions in Indian public opinion, as had the threat from Pakistan prior to the Bangladesh war. The external menace remained, though its source was redefined.

Contemporaneously there continues to exist the so-called politics of scarcity. The competition over shares tends to revolve around primary solidarities that get ranged against one another: clan versus clan, region versus region, state versus state. In this crucible the allocation of scarce resources comes to be an exercise in futility, in imagination, or in daring, but hardly in rationality.

At the same time recent years have been a period of rapid and stressful social change and of change from tradition to modernity. The latter is but poorly understood as a process and requires much more systematic analysis than it has so far received, but it is obvious that the changes that have taken place are uneven, haphazard, and incomplete, and so the transition has been even more traumatic.[84] It is also obvious that some sectors of society and the

---

[84] For a very good study of recent changes in India, see André Betaille, *Caste, Class and Power* (Berkeley, 1965), and M. N. Srinivas, *Social Change in Modern India* (Berkeley, 1966). See also Harold Gould, "Preliminary Observations concerning the Anthropology of Industrialization," *Eastern Anthropologist*, 14 (1960): 30–

economy have been much more substantially affected by modernizing changes than have others. This has been true for a variety of reasons, one of which has been that certain segments of society have been in closer juxtaposition to modernizing inputs and/or more receptive to such inputs. These changes are, however, so recent and fluid that they are only now beginning to be properly studied and have not as yet passed into the historian's province. If the historian can ask the right questions about how these processes came into being and what the significant factors were, he will have made a valuable contribution to understanding them.

47; Harold Gould, "Toward a 'Jati Model' for Indian Politics," *Economic and Political Weekly*, Feb. 1, 1969, pp. 1-6; and Richard Fox, "Avatars of Indian Research," *Comparative Studies in Society and History*, 12 (1970): 59-72. W. N. Brown, "Traditional Culture and Modern Developments in India," in *Report of the XI International Congress of the Historical Sciences* (Stockholm, 1960), 129-62, contains a fruitful discussion, especially of change in literature, belles-lettres, and the arts. See also Rudolph and Rudolph, *The Modernity of Tradition*.